Bali And Lombok Travel Guide

Your Ultimate Guide to Places to Visit, Things to Do, Tips, and Everything You Need to Know

Calder Quinn

Table Of Contents

Introduction

Why Bali?

Bali stands as a coveted destination that appears on the travel wish list of every passionate explorer. This is rightfully so, as the island not only mesmerizes with its stunning beauty but also possesses a rich cultural heritage, a diverse variety of plant and animal life, a vibrant culinary scene, and an overall tranquil atmosphere that appeals to both individuals traveling alone and groups of adventurers. Here are the reasons why Bali remains one of the most highly desired locations among globetrotters.

- **Exciting Volcanic Experiences**

For those in search of adventure, Bali's northeastern region is the ultimate spot. What could be more thrilling than ascending an active volcano? Mt. Batur and Mt. Agung, two significant active volcanoes, stand out as the main attractions. Undertaking a sunrise hike to the crater of Mt. Agung takes around five to seven hours, an endeavor that is well worth the experience. It's worth noting that Mt. Agung's most recent eruption occurred in 2017, while Mt. Batur's last eruption was in 2000. Climbing to the crater of Mt. Batur requires a minimum of eight hours.

- **Bird Enthusiasts' Delight**

Bali boasts an impressive variety of birds, with approximately 280 different species. The critically endangered Bali Starling is particularly remarkable, with fewer than 100 adults remaining in their natural habitat. Observing these exceptionally rare birds in the wild is a top priority for birdwatchers. If luck is on your side, you may come across these species exclusively in the forests of West Bali National Park and Nusa Penida.

- **Bali's Cultural Legacy**

Are you aware that Bali's unique Subak water management system has earned recognition as a UNESCO World Heritage Site?

The picturesque rice terraces that adorn Bali's landscapes owe their beauty to this ancient method of water management. This iconic system dates back to the ninth century and has become an essential element in the photo collections of every visitor to Bali.

- **Savor the World's Most Expensive Brew**

"Have faith in the process" is the motto of Kopi Luwak, a brew that demands attention. A single cup of this coffee can cost you approximately $40. Around the world, many enthusiasts are intrigued by this distinctive creation. In Bali, a creature resembling a cat, known as the luwak, consumes coffee cherries and later excretes the beans. The collected beans go through processes like roasting, grinding, and brewing/packaging, resulting in a unique experience that's truly worth sharing.

- **Mythical Charms of Komodo Island**

The island's name is inspired by the colossal Komodo Dragon, the largest lizard on Earth. Komodo Island, nestled within the Komodo National Park between Sumbawa and Flores, is home to this formidable creature. Covering an area of 390 square kilometers, the island isn't for the faint of heart, as it's inhabited by venomous Komodo dragons that can become aggressive if provoked. To avoid unwelcome encounters, it's best not to disturb these creatures. Additionally, Komodo Island boasts pink beaches, a captivating trait shared with only a few other places globally.

- **Underwater Encounters with Manta Rays**

Given Indonesia's expansive collection of over 17,000 islands, scuba diving naturally emerges as a popular activity. Bali's immaculate beaches, clear waters, and vibrant coral reefs support a diverse marine ecosystem. The opportunity to swim alongside manta rays adds an extra thrill to scuba diving adventures. In terms of expenses, anticipate scuba diving costs in Bali ranging from $60 to $80, which includes the necessary scuba gear.

- **Embark on Culinary Journeys in Bali**

To genuinely embrace Bali's culture and its role as a cultural hub, immerse yourself in the local culinary scene. From the renowned Babi Guling, a whole roasted pig, to the distinctive Nasi Jinggo served in banana leaf cones, and the iconic satay, Bali offers a diverse range of gastronomic experiences. Even for those following a vegetarian diet, Bali has options like the popular Gado-Gado salad, a delightful choice when prawn crackers are omitted. Opt for Nasi Goreng without meat, and you'll be treated to a delicious vegetarian version.

- **Bali Is An Affordable Getaway**

Bali demonstrates that a captivating destination doesn't have to strain your finances. The island features a cost-effective and efficient local transportation system, numerous guest houses offering accommodations for around $10 per night, and a multitude of local eateries catering to both vegetarian and non-vegetarian preferences. This affordability makes Bali an excellent choice for solo travelers as well.

- **The Splendor of Bali's Temples**

Bali's temples are truly iconic and draw the gaze of every photographer. The remarkable architecture of Balinese temples designates them as open-air places of worship, often bordered by intricately adorned gates and walls. These temples possess a distinctive allure that adds to the enchantment of Bali.

When To Go To Bali

As a passionate traveler, I'm eager to share an insider's perspective on the optimal times to explore Bali. This captivating Indonesian island offers a variety of experiences throughout the year. Your choice of when to visit can significantly influence the weather, crowds, and overall atmosphere of your journey.

1. Dry Season (April to September):

Bali's dry season stands out as the prime time to visit, and for good reason. Extending from April to September, this period delivers consistently warm and delightful weather. Skies are generally clear, and rainfall is minimal, making it ideal for outdoor pursuits, relaxing on the beach, and discovering the island's numerous attractions.

Pros:
- Sunshine-filled days and pleasant temperatures create the perfect environment for beach activities, water sports, and exploring.

- This timeframe experiences fewer weather-related interruptions to your plans.

- The dry season is excellent for diving and snorkeling, with superb visibility in the crystal-clear waters.

Cons:
- This is also the peak tourist season, resulting in larger crowds and elevated costs for accommodations and activities.

- Well-known tourist spots can become quite crowded, so it's advisable to book accommodations and activities well in advance.

2. Shoulder Seasons (October to November and February to March):

Bali's shoulder seasons, spanning from October to November and February to March, serve as the transitional periods between the island's wet and dry seasons. During these months, you'll find a middle ground between the bustling crowds of the dry season and the heavier rainfall of the wet season.

Pros:
- Accommodation and activity prices are generally more affordable compared to the peak dry season.

- The weather is relatively pleasant, with occasional brief showers.

- The island is less crowded, offering a more serene and authentic experience.

Cons
- While these months strike a good balance, there's still a possibility of rain, so packing a light raincoat or umbrella is recommended.

- Some attractions might operate with reduced hours or undergo maintenance during these quieter shoulder seasons.

3. Wet Season (December to January):

Bali's wet season encompasses December and January, characterized by increased rainfall and higher humidity levels. While this might not align with the iconic Bali postcard image, it presents a distinct opportunity for a unique exploration of the island.

Pros:
- Frequent rainfall lends a lush and vibrant appearance to the landscape.
- Accommodation prices often drop, and you might come across special deals.
- With fewer tourists around, attractions are less crowded, creating a more tranquil environment.

Cons:
- Consistent rainfall can lead to flooding and occasional travel disruptions.
- Activities involving beaches and water might be limited due to rough seas and unpredictable weather.

Determining the ideal time to visit Bali hinges on your preferences and priorities. For sunlit days, outdoor escapades, and a lively ambiance, the dry season from April to September is the prime choice. However, if you lean towards a more laid-back vibe, budget-friendly options, and occasional showers, the shoulder seasons present a well-rounded experience. Even the wet season possesses its allure for those who wish to explore Bali in a peaceful and contemplative setting. Regardless of your chosen time, Bali's rich heritage, breathtaking landscapes, and warm hospitality are certain to leave an enduring imprint on your journey.

Things You Must Not Miss

When you set out to explore the captivating island of Bali, you'll discover an array of unforgettable experiences awaiting your discovery. From pristine beaches to cultural marvels, here's a comprehensive list of things you absolutely must not miss during your Bali adventure:

1. Ubud and Its Surroundings: Immerse yourself in the cultural heart of Bali by venturing into Ubud. Pay a visit to the iconic Monkey Forest, delve into the Ubud Palace, and wander through the bustling Ubud Market. Make sure to also explore the Tegallalang Rice Terraces and the sacred Goa Gajah (Elephant Cave) located nearby.

2. Uluwatu Temple and Kecak Dance: Marvel at the breathtaking Uluwatu Temple, perched dramatically on a cliff with stunning ocean vistas. In the evening, catch the enchanting Kecak Dance performance set against the backdrop of the sun dipping below the horizon.

3. Tanah Lot Temple: Another iconic temple, Tanah Lot, stands gracefully on a rocky outcrop in the sea. Experience its magic during sunset for a truly enchanting moment.

4. Bali's Pristine Beaches: Relax on the idyllic shores of Bali, including well-known spots like Kuta, Seminyak, and Nusa Dua. For a quieter experience, seek out hidden treasures like Balangan Beach or Bingin Beach.

5. **Mount Batur Sunrise Trek**: Embark on an early morning trek to the peak of Mount Batur for an awe-inspiring sunrise view. The effort is richly rewarded by the sight that unfolds before you.

6. **Water Temples:** Discover Bali's water temples, such as Tirta Empul, where you can engage in a traditional purification ritual in the sacred spring pools.

7. **Bali Swing:** Satiate your spirit of adventure by taking a swing ride that soars high above the lush jungles of Ubud, providing a one-of-a-kind and exhilarating perspective.

8. **Experience Luwak Coffee**: Engage in the distinctive opportunity to taste Kopi Luwak, recognized as the world's most expensive coffee, produced through an unconventional process involving civet cats.

9. **Tegallalang Rice Terraces**: Take a stroll through the captivating terraced rice fields of Tegallalang, which showcase the agricultural beauty that Bali is known for.

10. **Water Adventures in Nusa Dua:** Dive into exhilarating water sports, ranging from snorkeling and scuba diving to parasailing and jet skiing, in the turquoise waters of Nusa Dua.

11. **Sacred Monkey Forest Sanctuary**: Playfully interact with the lively long-tailed macaques as you explore the lush sanctuary nestled within Ubud.

12. **Jatiluwih Rice Terraces**: Uncover the UNESCO-listed Jatiluwih Rice Terraces, celebrated for their breathtaking beauty and the distinctive subak irrigation system.

13. **Attend Temples during Galungan and Kuningan**: If your visit aligns with these Balinese festivals, revel in the island adorned

with intricate penjor decorations and join in the vibrant celebrations.

14. **Explore the Gili Islands**: Embark on a boat excursion to the nearby Gili Islands for a unique paradise experience, characterized by crystal-clear waters and vibrant marine life.

15. **Delight in Balinese Cuisine**: Indulge in the flavors of the region, including Nasi Goreng (fried rice), Babi Guling (roast pig), and Bebek Betutu (slow-cooked duck).

16. **Traditional Balinese Dance Performances**: Immerse yourself in captivating traditional dance shows like Barong and Legong, which vividly showcase the island's culturally rich heritage.

17. **Relaxation and Wellness**: Bali's reputation for spa and wellness offerings shines through. Treat yourself to traditional massages, spa treatments, and revitalizing yoga sessions.

18. **Explore the Underwater Realm:** Plunge into Bali's clear waters for snorkeling or diving adventures, where you'll witness vibrant coral reefs, underwater caves, and a diverse array of marine life.

19. **Tegenungan Waterfall**: Refresh yourself with a dip in the cascading waters of Tegenungan Waterfall, a picturesque natural wonder.

20. **Discover Local Markets and Artistry:** Roam through local markets and galleries to uncover intricate Balinese art, crafts, and souvenirs that hold sentimental value.

Bali unfolds as a destination that weaves a rich tapestry of experiences, each more captivating than the last. By immersing yourself in these activities and attractions, you'll undoubtedly craft cherished memories that will linger long after you've departed from this enchanting island.

Itinerary

Day 1: Arrival in Bali
- Arrive at Ngurah Rai International Airport.

- Find your way to your selected accommodation in Seminyak or Kuta.

- Take time to relax and explore the nearby beach, followed by dinner by the shore.

Day 2: Exploring Seminyak and Kuta
- Begin your day with an optional morning yoga session at your place of stay.

- Head to Double Six Beach for swimming and sunbathing.

- Discover the stylish boutiques and shops in Seminyak.

- Enjoy a delightful seafood dinner on the beach.

Day 3: Immersion in Ubud's Culture

- Depart for Ubud.

- Explore the renowned Ubud Monkey Forest.

- Visit the Ubud Market and Ubud Palace.

- Experience the captivating Tegallalang Rice Terraces.

- Conclude the day with an evening of traditional Balinese dance performance.

Day 4: Temples and Sunset
- Start by visiting Tirta Empul Water Temple for a unique purification ritual.

- Explore the ancient Gunung Kawi Temple.

- Proceed to Uluwatu Temple for the captivating Kecak Dance performance during sunset.

- End the day with a seafood dinner at the scenic Jimbaran Bay.

Day 5: Active Adventure

- Begin early with a trek up Mount Batur to witness a stunning sunrise.

- Enjoy breakfast with a view of the volcanic landscape.

- Relax at the Toya Devasya Hot Springs.

- Retire to your room and rest

Day 6: Nusa Dua Water Sports

- Depart for Nusa Dua.

- Engage in thrilling water sports including snorkeling, scuba diving, and parasailing.

- Unwind on Nusa Dua Beach.

- Return to Seminyak or Kuta in the evening.

Day 7: Cultural Delights and Departure

- Start your day by exploring the renowned Tanah Lot Temple, an iconic landmark that's a must-visit.

- Explore a traditional Balinese village and learn about local craftsmanship.

- Enjoy a farewell Balinese feast for lunch.

- Go to Ngurah Rai International Airport for your departure.

Please remember, that this is just a sample itinerary and you can adjust it according to your interests. Bali offers a wide range of attractions and activities, allowing you to create a unique and memorable journey.

Chapter 1: Brief Overview of Bali

History

Bali's rich history unfolds like a vibrant tapestry, woven with absorption, adoption, and adaptation—a reflection as vivid as its diverse culture and captivating landscape.

Emerging as the sea levels receded at the end of the Ice Age, the islands of Java and Bali became home for countless millennia. While evidence of human presence in Java dates back around 1.7 million years, Bali's oldest artifacts, stone tools found in Trunyan village, indicate human habitation around 202,000 years ago.

Around 2000 BC, Bali's allure attracted settlers from Java and distant regions such as Assam, Yunnan, and Tibet. This era of Neolithic migrations was soon accompanied by the opening of trade routes with influential civilizations like China and India.

Traces of significant cultural exchange between China and Bali became more apparent around 500 AD. By 700 AD, island states were embracing governance systems that originated in India. The earliest written inscriptions discovered in Bali, primarily of a Buddhist nature, date back to the 8th century. The roots of Hinduism also began to take hold around the 7th century.

Bali's historical landscape witnessed a series of conquests, including the notable Majapahit rule in 1343 AD. This period marked the beginning of an independent era, as Bali became a refuge for the Javanese aristocracy escaping political turmoil. This influence left a deep imprint on Bali's arts, culture, and religious practices, notably shaping the distinct form of Hinduism observed on the island.

The 16th century saw the arrival of European traders on Bali's shores, with the Portuguese leading the way. Bali's monarchs, practicing diplomacy, allowed the establishment of trading posts and formed strategic alliances with neighboring islands. Following the 17th-century invasion of Lombok, Bali experienced fragmentation, leading to the emergence of nine separate kingdoms.

Bali's historical records document the extensive Dutch military campaigns that began in 1846. Despite spirited resistance from the Balinese, these efforts resulted in significant sacrifices and eventual Dutch control. In 1942, Bali fell under Japanese occupation, which lasted until the end of World War II. After Japan's surrender, Indonesia boldly declared its independence under the leadership of Sukarno.

In the present day, Bali remains a cherished province within Indonesia, intricately entwined with the nation's identity. The province is subdivided into eight regencies and the Denpasar municipality, aligning with the historical boundaries of the Balinese kingdoms that existed before Indonesia declared independence in 1945.

Bali's history, characterized by a continuous interplay of cultural influences and the local community's resilience, forms an essential aspect of the island's allure. From its ancient beginnings to more recent chapters, the echoes of Bali's past resonate throughout its contemporary landscape, captivating travelers with narratives of determination, heritage, and evolution.

Culture

Bali's culture weaves a rich tapestry of ancient customs, vibrant rituals, intricate artistic expressions, and a profound spiritual core. The cultural fabric of this Indonesian island creates a symphony of colors, sounds, flavors, and beliefs, resulting in a captivating and harmonious experience for all who venture to explore it.

1. Spirituality and Religion: At the heart of Balinese culture lies its distinctive form of Hinduism, deeply rooted in indigenous beliefs and practices. The island is adorned with intricate temples, each carrying its meaning and purpose. Daily rituals, ceremonies, and offerings infuse every corner with a sense of devotion.

2. Dance and Performance: Balinese dance serves as a captivating cultural expression, portraying mythical tales and historical narratives. The mesmerizing combination of intricate hand movements, vibrant costumes, and rhythmic music creates a captivating spectacle. Traditional dances such as Barong, Legong, and Kecak enchant audiences with their grace and dramatic flair.

3. Music and Gamelan: The haunting melodies of the Balinese gamelan orchestra resonate across the island. Comprising an array of percussion instruments, gongs, and metallophones, the gamelan accompanies ceremonies, dances, and theatrical performances, transporting listeners to a different realm.

4. Visual Arts and Craftsmanship: Balinese artistry is celebrated globally for its meticulous craftsmanship and spiritual essence. Paintings, wood carvings, stone sculptures, and textiles reflect the island's mythologies and philosophies. Ubud, a cultural hub, is a treasure trove of galleries and studios.

5. Festivals and Celebrations: Bali's calendar is adorned with vibrant festivals, known as "odalan" or "pura," dedicated to temple anniversaries. The Galungan festival, symbolizing the triumph of dharma over adharma, is a highlight, characterized by ornately adorned bamboo poles.

6. Traditional Architecture: The island's architecture showcases intricate designs, often featuring open pavilions, courtyards, and meticulously carved stone motifs. Balinese compounds seamlessly blend with nature, reflecting a deep reverence for the environment.

7. **Rice Terraces and Subak System**: Beyond their agricultural significance, the breathtaking rice terraces embody Balinese cultural values. The subak system, a UNESCO World Heritage Site, governs irrigation and symbolizes community collaboration.

8. **Wayang Kulit Puppetry**: Wayang Kulit, the art of shadow puppetry, offers entrancing storytelling. Elaborately crafted leather puppets cast shadows on illuminated screens, reenacting epics like the Ramayana.

9. **Traditional Cuisine:** Balinese culinary delights tantalize palates with distinct flavors and aromatic herbs and spices. Dishes like Babi Guling (roast pig), Bebek Betutu (slow-cooked duck), and Lawar (spiced meat dish) provide a culinary adventure.

10. **Community and Harmony**: The concept of "gotong royong," communal cooperation, is deeply embedded in Balinese culture. It fosters unity and ensures the collective well-being of the community.

The culture of Bali is a living entity, a dynamic blend of tradition and modernity. It's a celebration of life, nature, and spiritual exploration, inviting travelers to immerse themselves in its beauty and embark on a truly transformative journey.

Geography

Bali's enchanting geography paints a vibrant picture of diverse landscapes, ranging from pristine beaches to lush terraced rice fields and towering volcanic peaks. Nestled within Indonesia's sprawling archipelago, Bali's unique topography has left an indelible mark on its ecosystems, cultures, and way of life.

1. **Origins in Volcanism:** Bali's captivating topography is a product of its volcanic past. As an integral part of the Pacific Ring of Fire, the island boasts a collection of volcanoes. The majestic Mount Agung, an active stratovolcano, not only graces the skyline but also holds deep spiritual significance.

2. **Coastal Allure**: Bali's coastlines offer a paradise for beach enthusiasts. Along the southern shore, stretches like Kuta, Legian, and Seminyak unveil golden sands and lively nightlife. The eastern coast unveils quieter black sand havens such as Amed and Tulamben, an underwater paradise for divers and snorkelers.

3. **Heartland of Highlands**: Bali's core showcases emerald terraced rice fields and rolling hills. Nestled within these highlands is Ubud, renowned for its artistic charm, cultural vitality, and breathtaking vistas.

4. **Tranquil North**: The northern coastline extends an invitation to serenity. Lovina Beach

boasts black sands and the chance to encounter playful dolphins. In the Singaraja region, colonial architecture and echoes of history await exploration.

5. **West Bali's Biodiversity**: The West Bali National Park is a sanctuary embracing both land and sea. It embraces mangroves, monsoon forests, and vibrant coral reefs, providing a haven for unique wildlife, including the critically endangered Bali Starling.

6. **The Nusa Escape**: To the southeast lie the Nusa islands—Nusa Penida, Nusa Lembongan, and Nusa Ceningan. These untouched gems offer crystalline waters, towering cliffs, and an underwater realm teeming with life.

7. **Vibrant Coral Gardens**: Bali's coastal waters host thriving coral reefs, forming a haven for divers and snorkelers alike. Dive sites such as the USS Liberty shipwreck at Tulamben and Menjangan Island's marine reserve stand as a testament to this underwater wonderland.

8. **Subak's Water Symphony**: The iconic terraced rice fields owe their beauty to the Subak irrigation system, designated a UNESCO World Heritage Site. This intricate network of canals and weirs embodies Bali's harmonious rapport with nature.

9. **Natural Treasures**: Bali's interior conceals hidden treasures—caves to explore and waterfalls to behold. Goa Gajah (Elephant Cave) and Tegenungan Waterfall are just a glimpse into this captivating world.

10. **Bali's Climate Tale**: Bali basks in a tropical climate, defined by distinct wet and dry seasons. The dry season, from April to September, offers sun-kissed days, while the wet season, from October to March, brings life-nurturing rains and lush landscapes.

11. **Flourishing Flora and Fauna:** Bali's diverse ecosystems harbor a myriad of plant and animal species, from swaying coconut palms to

lively monkeys and vibrant birds. The Bali Myna, a symbol of conservation efforts, underlines the island's commitment to preserving its natural wealth.

12. **Embracing Batur Caldera**: The expansive Batur Caldera cradles Lake Batur, Bali's largest lake. This scenic wonderland also offers trekking trails for explorers seeking panoramic vistas.

13. **Mangroves**: Along the southern coasts, vital mangrove forests thrive, serving as crucial breeding grounds for marine life and offering a chance for eco-conscious travelers to engage in meaningful experiences.

Bali's geography not only showcases its natural allure but also underscores its influence on the island's cultural legacy. Beyond its breathtaking landscapes, Bali's essence is a fusion of its people, land, and sea—a living canvas waiting to be explored and experienced.

Religion

Religion bears profound significance in Bali, interweaving through every facet of daily existence—from rituals to art and governance. Predominantly, Balinese Hinduism holds sway, an extraordinary fusion of indigenous beliefs, ancient customs, and Hindu influences. This spiritual bedrock molds the island's cultural essence, nurturing a profound bond between its people, traditions, and the divine.

1. **Balinese Hinduism**: With roots in ancient animistic practices, Balinese Hinduism forms a vivid mosaic of rituals, ceremonies, and beliefs. Reverence is directed toward gods, goddesses, spirits, and ancestors, each playing a distinct role within the island's cosmic tapestry.

2. **Temples**: Bali's canvas is adorned with myriad temples, ranging from stately complexes to humble shrines. The Mother Temple, Pura Besakih, gracing Mount Agung's slopes, holds profound spiritual sway. These sanctuaries aren't

solely places of devotion; they also serve as artistic, dance, and communal hubs.

3. **Offerings**: "Canang sari," the daily offerings, are integral to Balinese life. These intricate compositions of flowers, rice, and symbolic tokens are presented to honor and appease deities, spirits, and forebears.

4. **Ceremonies**: Bali's calendar is punctuated by an array of ceremonies and festivals, commemorating life's milestones, agriculture, and the spiritual realm. The Galungan festival, celebrating the victory of good over evil, is marked by exquisitely adorned bamboo poles.

5. **Dance and Drama**: Balinese dance and drama transcend mere performance, evolving into acts of devotion. Mythic tales and historical chronicles come alive through intricate gestures, vibrant attire, and rhythmic melodies.

6. **Subak System**: The UNESCO-designated Subak system embodies the harmony between

religion, culture, and nature. This communal irrigation framework sustains Bali's lush rice terraces, embodying cooperation and equilibrium.

7. **Karma and Dharma:** Core tenets of Balinese Hinduism encompass karma (action and consequence) and dharma (righteous duty). Individuals strive to fulfill their dharma, accumulating positive karma to ascend spiritually.

8. **Caste System**: Bali's caste system, more flexible than its Indian counterpart, still influences social dynamics. Brahmins (priests and scholars), Kshatriyas (warriors and rulers), Vaishyas (merchants and farmers), and Shudras (laborers) shape the four primary castes.

9. **Role of Priests**: Balinese priests, known as "pedandas," are revered mentors in religious and spiritual matters. They conduct ceremonies, offer blessings, and provide insights into the intricate world of Hindu philosophy.

10. **Spirituality in Daily Life**: Balinese Hinduism transcends temples and rituals, permeating daily life. Offerings are crafted meticulously, ceremonies observed dutifully, and harmony with nature maintained in reverence to the divine.

11. **Conservation of Sacred Sites**: Balinese Hindus hold their natural surroundings in deep veneration. Mountains, lakes, forests, and coastlines are sanctified, fostering preservation endeavors.

In Bali, religion thrives as a vibrant, living tradition that shapes values, norms, and interactions. The island's spiritual core radiates through customs, arts, and landscapes, beckoning visitors to engage in a culture steeped in reverence and devotion.

Language

The primary language spoken in Bali is Balinese, an Austronesian language with distinct dialects and nuances that reflect the island's rich cultural heritage. However, due to Bali's popularity as a tourist destination, English has become widely spoken, especially in tourist areas and among those in the hospitality industry. This linguistic diversity contributes to the island's dynamic atmosphere and ease of communication for visitors from around the world.

1. **Balinese Language**: Balinese, rooted in the Austronesian language family, is characterized by complex grammar, honorifics, and a system of politeness levels. It holds cultural significance and is used in rituals, ceremonies, and traditional performances.

2. **Dialects**: Different regions within Bali have their Balinese dialects, each with unique pronunciation, vocabulary, and grammatical variations. This reflects the island's diverse communities and local identities.

3. **Indonesian Language (Bahasa Indonesia)**: As Indonesia's national language, Bahasa Indonesia is also widely spoken and understood in Bali. It unifies various ethnic groups in the country and is used for official communication, education, and media.

4. **English**: English is common in Bali, particularly in tourist areas like Kuta, Seminyak, Ubud, and Nusa Dua. Many locals in the hospitality and tourism sectors are proficient in English to serve international visitors.

5. **Multilingualism**: Bali's linguistic landscape is multicultural. Alongside Balinese, Indonesian, and English, you might hear other languages spoken by tourists and expatriates, enriching diversity.

6. **Cultural Interactions**: Learning basic Balinese or Indonesian phrases enhances interactions and demonstrates respect. Simple greetings like "Selamat pagi" (Good morning)

and "Terima kasih" (Thank you) foster positive connections.

7. **Signs and Information**: In tourist areas, signs, menus, and information are often provided in English and Indonesian, aiding navigation and communication.

8. **Language of Hospitality**: While various languages are present, hospitality's language is universal. Smiles, gratitude, and respectful gestures transcend barriers and create meaningful connections.

In Bali, language bridges cultures, connecting people from diverse backgrounds. Whether exploring Balinese dialects or using English, the linguistic tapestry enhances immersing in the vibrant culture.

Food And Drinks

Bali's culinary landscape is a delectable journey through flavors, textures, and traditions. With a rich blend of local ingredients, cultural influences, and culinary creativity, the island's food and drinks offer a tantalizing experience for every palate.

1. **Balinese Cuisine**: Balinese cuisine is a symphony of aromatic herbs, spices, and fresh ingredients. Dishes are often prepared with a combination of sweet, sour, salty, and spicy flavors. Staples include rice, vegetables, meat, and seafood.

2. **Babi Guling:** A signature dish, Babi Guling is a succulent roasted pig stuffed with a fragrant blend of herbs and spices. It's a culinary masterpiece often served during special occasions and celebrations.

3. **Nasi Goreng and Mie Goreng**: Nasi Goreng (fried rice) and Mie Goreng (fried noodles) are staples found in local eateries and international menus alike. These dishes are a canvas for various toppings and protein choices.

4. **Lawar**: Lawar is a traditional dish made from minced meat, vegetables, and rich spices. It's a harmonious blend of flavors, often served during ceremonies and festivities.

5. **Sate**: Balinese sate, or satay, features skewered and grilled meat (chicken, pork, or fish) served with a flavorful peanut sauce. It's a popular street food and a delicious snack.

6. **Seafood**: Being an island, Bali offers a bounty of fresh seafood. Grilled fish, prawns, and squid dishes are commonly found along the coastal areas.

7. **Vegetarian Options**: Bali caters well to vegetarian preferences. Dishes like Gado-Gado (vegetable salad with peanut sauce) and Nasi Campur (mixed rice with vegetables and tofu) are delightful options.

8. **Balinese Sambal**: Sambal, a spicy chili paste, is a condiment that accompanies many dishes. It adds a fiery kick and enhances the overall flavor.

9. **Exotic Fruits**: Bali's tropical climate yields an array of exotic fruits like snake fruit, salak, mangosteen, and rambutan. Don't miss the opportunity to savor these refreshing treats.

10. **Traditional Drinks**: Try traditional drinks like "Jamu," an herbal concoction believed to have healing properties, and "Arak," a locally distilled spirit often used as a base for cocktails.

11. **Luwak Coffee**: Bali is famous for producing Luwak coffee, one of the world's most expensive and unique brews. The coffee beans are consumed and excreted by civets, enhancing the flavor profile.

12. **Beachfront Dining:** Bali's beachfront areas offer an array of dining options, from casual beach shacks serving seafood to upscale restaurants with ocean views.

13. **Cooking Classes**: Joining a cooking class in Bali is a delightful way to learn about the

island's culinary heritage. You can learn to prepare traditional dishes and gain insights into local cooking techniques.

14. **Tropical Fruit Juices**: Sip on tropical fruit juices and smoothies made from fresh ingredients like mango, pineapple, and coconut, providing a refreshing respite from the tropical heat.

From street food stalls to elegant restaurants, Bali's food scene caters to every taste. Whether you're indulging in traditional Balinese fare or exploring international cuisine, each dish and drink reflects the island's vibrant culture and the creativity of its culinary artisans.

Festival And Events

Bali's vibrant cultural calendar is adorned with a myriad of festivals and events that illuminate the island with colors, music, dance, and spiritual devotion. These celebrations offer a glimpse into

Balinese traditions, beliefs, and the joyous spirit of its people.

1. **Galungan and Kuningan**: Galungan marks the triumph of good over evil, and Kuningan signifies the end of the Galungan period. Elaborate offerings, bamboo poles adorned with decorations, and festive processions are integral to these celebrations.

2. **Nyepi (Day of Silence)**: Nyepi is a unique cultural phenomenon where the entire island comes to a standstill. Bali's Hindu population observes a day of silence, fasting, and self-reflection. No lights, activities, or travel are allowed, creating a serene atmosphere.

3. **Saraswati**: Saraswati celebrates knowledge, learning, and the arts. Balinese temples are adorned with offerings and books, reflecting the importance of education in the culture.

4. **Tumpek Landep**: This event honors metal objects, such as tools and weapons. Blessings are

offered to these items to imbue them with positive energy and enhance their usefulness.

5. **Odalan**: Odalan refers to temple anniversaries, celebrated with vibrant processions, dance performances, and communal feasts. Each temple has its anniversary date, contributing to Bali's bustling festival calendar.

6. **Pagerwesi**: Pagerwesi emphasizes spiritual protection against negative influences. It's a time to fortify oneself against negative energies through prayers and rituals.

7. **Kite Festival**: Bali's skies come alive with colorful kites during the Kite Festival. This event showcases intricate kites of various shapes and sizes, accompanied by friendly competitions.

8. **Ubud Writers and Readers Festival**: This literary event attracts writers, scholars, and book enthusiasts from around the world. It's a

platform for thought-provoking discussions, workshops, and cultural exchanges.

9. **Bali Arts Festival**: Held annually, this month-long festival celebrates Bali's artistic heritage. Dance performances, traditional music, craft exhibitions, and culinary delights captivate visitors.

10. **Makepung Buffalo Races**: Witness the excitement of buffalo races in West Bali. Farmers gather for friendly competitions, showcasing their decorated buffaloes and traditional jockeys.

11. **Piodalan**: Piodalan is a temple ceremony that signifies the anniversary of a family temple. It's a time for prayers, offerings, and community gatherings.

12. **Ubud Food Festival**: This gastronomic event celebrates Indonesian cuisine, featuring cooking demonstrations, culinary workshops, and discussions on food sustainability.

13. **Baliem Valley Festival**: In Papua, the Baliem Valley Festival offers a glimpse into the indigenous cultures of Papua through traditional music, dance, and rituals.

14. **Waisak (Vesak):** Although not unique to Bali, Waisak holds significance. It commemorates the birth, enlightenment, and passing of Buddha. Devotees participate in processions and light candles as an act of devotion.

Bali's festivals and events immerse visitors in the island's vibrant cultural tapestry. These occasions provide insights into Balinese spirituality, artistry, and community bonds, inviting travelers to partake in the joyous celebrations and witness the island's traditions come to life.

Chapter 2: How To Prepare For Your Trip To Bali

During the rainy season, continuous rainfall is not common, but frequent and consistent rain occurs, accompanied by high humidity levels. It's important to note that this is not the monsoon pattern observed in other Asian countries.

To avoid encountering a large number of tourists, it's best to steer clear of July and August, which see a surge in mass tourism.

For favorable weather conditions, it's recommended to plan your trip during the dry period from May to November.

If you want to experience milder temperatures, consider traveling in July, which is the coldest month of the year with temperatures around 23°C or 73.4°F.

Determining the duration of your stay in Bali is also crucial. Keep in mind several factors, including your budget and the size of the island.

Bali spans approximately 150 kilometers (93 miles) from east to west and covers an area of 5,630 km² (2173 mi²). Despite its cultural significance, Bali isn't a particularly large island.

A stay of 15 days to 4 weeks is ideal for exploring Bali thoroughly. It's advisable to avoid trips shorter than 15 days to prevent a rushed experience. Remember, you're on vacation, so take your time and enjoy the laid-back atmosphere.

For those fortunate enough, a month-long stay offers a more immersive experience of Balinese culture and life.

Regardless of the duration, try not to overextend your itinerary. Although Bali is relatively small, travel times can be longer due to traffic and congestion. It's common to spend an hour in traffic covering just 15 kilometers (9 miles), so keep this in mind when planning.

When searching for flights to Bali, remember that airfare is often a significant portion of your travel budget. Booking your flights 5 to 6 months in advance is recommended to secure the best rates.

At the moment, there are no direct flights from Europe or the USA to Ngurah Rai Airport in Denpasar, Bali. Layovers in major international cities are necessary, with flight durations lasting 17 to 25 hours. The preferred layover city depends on the chosen airline to Indonesia.

Various airlines connect Bali to different cities throughout the year. For flights from Europe, options include Singapore Airlines, Emirates, Qatar Airways, Cathay Pacific, Aeroflot, Thai Airways, China Southern, Korean Air, Oman Air, Malaysia Airlines, Turkish Airlines, and Etihad Airways. From Australia, carriers such as

Qantas, Jet Star, Virgin Australia, and Garuda Indonesia operate.

To secure the best airfare, utilize flight comparison platforms like Google Flights or Expedia. It's wise to make direct reservations through the airlines' official websites.

Remember that more layovers can lead to potential delays and missed connections, especially on long-haul flights.

Roundtrip flight costs to Bali differ, ranging from €700 to over €1300 per person from Europe in economy class, varying by season. From Australia, economy class prices are around AU$600.

Based on my experience, if departing from Europe (e.g., Paris), a cost-effective and practical option is the Paris-Charles de Gaulle (CDG) to Singapore route. This minimizes flight duration and provides access to a top airline. Then, consider taking an AirAsia flight from

Singapore to Denpasar. Air Asia is a reliable low-cost airline with regular flights.

Consider booking a multi-destination ticket for affordability. Reserving a Paris-Singapore flight and a separate Singapore-Bali ticket is often more economical than a single Paris-Bali ticket.

For those with a flexible budget, a 3 to 4-day layover in Singapore before reaching Bali can be rewarding. This allows exploration of the green city and better management of jet lag, ensuring a comfortable arrival in Bali.

Visa Entry And Requirements.

Travelers planning a trip to Bali should be aware of the visa entry and requirements to ensure a smooth and hassle-free journey. The Indonesian government has established guidelines to facilitate travel while maintaining security and compliance with immigration regulations.

1. **Visa Exemption**: Citizens of certain countries are eligible for visa exemption when visiting Bali for tourism purposes. This allows them to stay for up to 30 days without obtaining a visa. However, this period cannot be extended beyond the 30-day limit.

2. **Visa on Arrival (VoA):** Some nationalities can obtain a Visa on Arrival upon arriving in Bali. This allows for a stay of up to 30 days, with the option to extend for an additional 30 days. The Visa on Arrival is obtained at the immigration counter in the airport upon arrival.

3. **Tourist Visa:** For travelers who intend to stay in Bali for longer than 30 days, a tourist visa may be required. This visa can typically be obtained from an Indonesian embassy or consulate before traveling to Bali. It allows for a stay of up to 60 days, with the possibility of extending for an additional 30 days.

4. **Social and Business Visas**: Travelers visiting for social or business purposes may require a

different type of visa. The social visa allows for a longer stay, often up to 60 days, and can be extended within Indonesia. The business visa is intended for business-related activities and may also allow for an extended stay.

5. **Visa Extensions**: If your initial stay is approaching its expiration and you wish to extend your time in Bali, you may be able to apply for an extension. This process typically involves visiting an immigration office in Bali and providing the necessary documents and fees.

6. **Passport Validity**: Ensure that your passport is valid for at least six months beyond your intended departure date from Bali. Some airlines and immigration authorities may require this validity period.

7. **Document Requirements**: When entering Bali, travelers should have a valid passport, return or onward flight tickets, and proof of sufficient funds for their stay.

8. **Health and Travel Insurance**: While not a visa requirement, having health and travel insurance is highly recommended. It can provide coverage in case of unexpected medical expenses, trip cancellations, or emergencies.

9. **Overstay Fees**: Overstaying your visa can result in fines and other penalties. It's important to be aware of the duration of your permitted stay and to adhere to the immigration regulations.

10. **COVID-19 Entry Requirements:** Due to the ongoing global pandemic, entry requirements and regulations related to COVID-19 are subject to change. It's advisable to check the official website of the Indonesian immigration authorities or contact the nearest Indonesian embassy or consulate for the most up-to-date information before traveling.

Understanding the visa entry and requirements for Bali is essential for a smooth and enjoyable travel experience. Always verify the latest information with official sources to ensure compliance with immigration regulations.

Packing Essentials For Bali Climate

Preparing for Bali's tropical climate requires careful consideration of the island's warm temperatures, high humidity, and occasional rain showers. Here's a checklist of necessary items to pack for your trip, to ensure your comfort and readiness:

1. **Lightweight Clothing**: Pack breathable, lightweight clothes such as shorts, dresses, and airy tops. Opt for moisture-wicking fabrics that allow your skin to breathe.

2. **Swimsuits and Cover-ups**: Bali's stunning beaches and resorts make swimsuits a must. Remember to bring cover-ups for strolls beyond the water.

3. **Sun Protection**: Include high SPF sunscreen, sunglasses, and a wide-brimmed hat to shield yourself from Bali's strong sun.

4. **Mosquito Repellent**: Bali's tropical environment means mosquitos are around. Make sure you pack enough mosquito repellents to protect against insect bites.

5. **Rain Gear:** While rain showers are brief, they're common. Pack a compact umbrella or a lightweight rain jacket.

6. **Comfortable Shoes**: Bring comfortable walking shoes for exploring and sandals or flip-flops for beach visits.

7. **Light Layers**: Evenings can be cooler, so consider packing a light sweater or a long-sleeve shirt.

8. **Modest Attire**: If temple visits or ceremonies are planned, have modest clothing like a sarong or long skirt.

9. **Power Adapter**: Bali uses Type C and Type F electrical outlets. Ensure you bring suitable power adapters for your devices.

10. **Travel Essentials**: Don't forget your passport, travel insurance documents, necessary medications, and a compact first aid kit.

11. **Travel Documents**: Keep photocopies of your passport, visa, and other crucial documents in case of emergencies.

12. **Beach Accessories**: If beach time is on your agenda, pack a beach towel, beach bag, and any water-related gear like snorkeling equipment.

13. **Light Backpack**: A small, lightweight backpack can be handy for carrying essentials while exploring.

14. **Camera and Charger**: Capture Bali's beauty with your camera or smartphone. Remember chargers and extra batteries.

15. **Cash and Cards**: While credit cards are widely accepted, carry some local currency for small purchases and places that don't take cards.

16. **Medicine and Personal Care Items:** Pack prescription medications, basic first aid supplies, and personal care items you might need.

17. **Plug Adapters**: Bali uses European-style Type C and Type F plugs. Bring suitable plug adapters for charging your electronics.

18. **Casual Evening Wear**: For dinners or outings, pack a few casual evening outfits suitable for Bali's relaxed atmosphere.

By having these essentials on hand, you'll be well-equipped to enjoy Bali's tropical climate and make the most of your unforgettable trip.

Chapter 3: Transportation in Bali

Getting Around Bali

The most convenient way to explore Bali is by hiring a car and driver. This option provides the freedom to travel without the hassle of driving yourself. Biking is also possible, though be prepared for navigating through busy traffic. While boats are excellent for reaching neighboring islands, they are not commonly used for getting around Bali.

Most travelers arrive at Ngurah Rai International Airport (DPS), situated between Kuta and Jimbaran on the island's southern tip. To reach your hotel, check if there's a complimentary resort shuttle available. Some hotels offer private transportation for a fee, which can be worthwhile, especially if you arrive at night. The driver will know the exact drop-off point, a convenience some find worth the extra cost. If you choose a taxi, you'll prepay your fare at the airport's taxi counter. Fares vary widely depending on your destination, ranging from 45,000 rupiahs (about $3) to 315,000 rupiahs (approximately $22).

Bike

For short distances, using bikes is an inexpensive and enjoyable method to easily explore beyond your hotel. Biking can also be a quicker choice in towns with heavy traffic. You have the option to rent bicycles from a variety of resorts and small stores in tourist towns such as Kuta. Rental costs differ based on the company and the type of bike, ranging from 60,000 rupiahs (less than $5) to 350,000 rupiahs (about $24) per day. Bali Bike Rental, Bali Rides, and Bali Eco Cycling have all received positive feedback from previous visitors.

Because some of Bali's roads are not very stable, it's best to steer clear of biking in congested areas like Denpasar and Kuta.

Hired Car And Driver

This transportation option might appear extravagant initially, but you'll discover that it can be a cost-effective and worthwhile choice. Arranging a car and driver is often possible through your hotel, although various agencies like Bali Island Car Rental provide this service as well. Be prepared to negotiate the price (unless it's already arranged) and cover the driver's expenses for food, drinks, and accommodations if the hire is for multiple days. A day's car hire typically costs around $50. Despite the cost, you'll have a hassle-free way of getting around and potentially a local tour guide. For more details, you can consult your hotel's concierge, who might offer a similar service for a fee.

Rental Car

Renting a car is a straightforward and budget-friendly option, but navigating Bali's roads can be challenging due to traffic, driving habits, and unclear signs. Legally, you need an international driver's permit or a locally issued one. Rental companies like Hertz, Sixt, Avis, and Budget are available in various resort towns and at Ngurah Rai International Airport.

Taxi

Travelers' experiences with taxis in Bali can vary. While some drivers might be unreliable or attempt to deceive, fortunately, many are honest and welcoming to tourists. Different taxis operate either on negotiated prices or metered rates. Initial fares usually start at approximately 5,000 to 7,000 Indonesian rupiahs (around $0.50), with each additional kilometer costing 4,000 rupiahs (about $0.25). In larger towns like Denpasar, you can flag down cabs on the street or call for one. Among taxi operators, the Blue Bird Group is frequently praised for its reliability by travelers. The company even provides a smartphone app to simplify the process of finding an available cab.

Whether you're choosing Blue Bird Group or another taxi company on the island, it's important to follow some safety measures. Always ensure the driver uses the meter to ensure the correct fare and take a glance at a map to verify that your driver is taking the appropriate route.

Bus

Both public and private tour buses offer an economical means to explore the island. However, they may limit the flexibility to venture off the main routes and can be time-consuming to reach destinations. One of the well-known private bus tour organizers in Bali is Perama Tour & Travel.

Bali's public buses connect major towns, but information about routes, costs, departure, and arrival times can be challenging to find. The newer Kura-Kura public shuttle bus has received positive reviews; it operates on five lines connecting key tourist hubs such as Kuta, Seminyak, and Ubud. These buses feature amenities like free Wi-Fi, air conditioning, audio-visual announcements, and luggage racks. Keep in mind that they have infrequent schedules, with some routes departing every two hours. The fixed fares for single journeys range from 20,000 to 80,000 rupiah (approximately $1.50 to $5.50). Look for green and yellow buses adorned with cartoon turtles.

Boat

At times, travelers opt for boats and ferries to access nearby islands from Bali. This choice is not only picturesque but also budget-friendly. Although public ferries might be more economical, commercial boat services provided by companies like Perama Tour & Travel and Blue Water Express offer swift and direct transportation to the neighboring islands. Nevertheless, it's important to be aware that several boat operators might lack proper training and safety regulations might be lacking. It's advisable to consider that larger boats are generally safer, and travelers should also inspect safety equipment before embarking on boats.

Motorbike Taxi

In earlier times, unofficial motorbike taxis known as "ojeks," often operated by young men on street corners, were the common way to navigate Bali's towns. Nowadays, apps like Gojek and Grab have made finding an Ojek easier than ever.

For less familiar or challenging-to-pronounce addresses, you can simply drop a pin on your app for your destination, eliminating the need for complex explanations with your rider. Motorcycle taxi rides usually cost about half the price of a car ride. Riders always have spare helmets for passengers, and app codes of conduct keep them from the reckless driving that used to be common among daredevil ojek drivers. Similar to booking a car taxi, prices are fixed and shown before confirming your booking.

Keep in mind that some villages in Bali prohibit access to Grab and Gojek to safeguard the income of their local drivers. These restrictions might require you to walk a short distance to your final destination.

Accessible Transportation In Bali

For travelers with disabilities and mobility needs, Bali can pose challenges. Even in more developed tourist areas like Kuta, Ubud, Canggu, and Seminyak, sidewalks are often poorly maintained, and roads are narrow. However, access to many main attractions has improved, with the addition of wheelchair ramps at prominent temples and priority access for individuals with mobility requirements. Much of Ubud Monkey Forest, Tirta Gangga temple, the beautiful Pura Tirta Empul water temple, and even sections of the Jatiluwih paddy fields trails are wheelchair-accessible.

Chapter 4: Accommodation Options In Bali

Located in the Indian Ocean, Bali is just a brief ferry journey away from its neighboring giant, Java. However, this Hindu-majority island stands in stark contrast.

The essence of Balinese aesthetics flows through the very essence of this captivating land. Its exquisite temples showcase distinctive architecture, its eateries lure millennials with their Instagram-worthy interiors, and its wellness retreats usher in serenity the moment you step inside.

Renowned for its diverse offerings, including surfing, stunning beaches, vibrant nightlife, and exceptionally stylish design, Bali has something to captivate every type of visitor.

Whether you seek yoga sessions in off-the-beaten-path coastal villages, ride the waves in the bustling southwest beach havens, or unwind amidst the paradise of rice paddies in its hilly heartland, Bali offers a plethora of experiences.

Bali is situated in the Indian Ocean, just a short ferry ride away from its neighboring giant, Java. However, despite the proximity, this island, with its Hindu-majority population, stands out distinctly.

The essence of Balinese aesthetics is deeply ingrained in this fascinating land. Its temples showcase unique architectural styles, restaurants attract millennials with their visually appealing interiors, and wellness retreats offer an immediate sense of relaxation upon entry.

Bali is renowned for its wide-ranging attractions, including world-class surfing, picturesque beaches, vibrant nightlife, and chic design elements. No matter the type of traveler, Bali has something to offer. You can engage in yoga sessions in tranquil coastal villages, ride the waves in the energetic beachfront spots of the southwest, or unwind amidst the serene beauty of rice paddies in the island's hilly interior.

UBUD

Already renowned as a popular destination for backpackers and hippies, Ubud had gained fame even before "Eat, Pray, Love" transformed it into a magnet for those seeking self-discovery. Situated in the heart of Bali, Ubud is unique in that it lacks beaches. Instead, it offers breathtaking mountain vistas, lush jungle getaways, and the vivid green landscapes of rice terraces.

Ubud itself, nestled in the uplands, is essentially a collection of villages. It boasts a plethora of cafes, bars, craft shops, and restaurants. This locale is equally accommodating for backpackers, offering hostels and budget-friendly homestays, as it is for those in search of exclusive retreats – think tree houses nestled in rainforests and villas surrounded by rice terraces.

Additionally, if you opt to stay nearby, you'll have the chance to leisurely visit the Ubud Monkey Temple, where macaques abound.

Where To Stay In Ubud

LUXURY

ALAYA RESORT UBUD is a haven nestled amidst lush rice paddies and meticulously manicured gardens, offering a picturesque setting for relaxation. Guests can enjoy a range of facilities including a swimming pool, and fitness center, as well as a restaurant and bar with live music in the evenings. The elegantly designed rooms exude Balinese charm with intricate details and terraces that seamlessly merge with nature. This delightful 5-star retreat enjoys a prime location, near Ubud Monkey Forest and a short walk from Ubud Market.

ULUN UBUD RESORT: Nestled amid abundant tropical greenery and overlooking the Tjampuhan River, Ulun Ubud Resort provides a tranquil sanctuary. The ambient bedrooms are designed to induce relaxation, featuring four-poster beds, balconies, and a soothing neutral color palette. Some rooms even offer direct access to a swimming pool. The resort encompasses an Indonesian restaurant specializing in local cuisine, a lounge bar, and a library. Furthermore, a spa and wellness center offer an opportunity to unwind and rejuvenate. Situated in Sanggan Village, the resort's strategic location offers easy access to Ubud's center, facilitated by a complimentary shuttle service.

PAJAR HOUSE UBUD & VILLAS presents an array of accommodations, from rooms to villas, catering to diverse guest preferences. Each lodging features high rattan ceilings, white tiled floors, and four-poster beds. Some even offer outdoor bathrooms, immersing guests in nature's embrace. With a 3-star rating, the property offers landscaped gardens complementing an outdoor swimming pool. Guests can freely explore the vicinity or dine at nearby eateries using the hotel's complimentary bike rentals. For instance, the Ubud Botanic Gardens are a mere two kilometers away, and the hotel extends the convenience of a free shuttle bus service to Ubud.

SEMINYAK

Seminyak exudes its unique charm as a contrast to the vibrant party scene of Legian and the urban atmosphere of Kuta. This sophisticated enclave offers an elevated experience in terms of dining, beverages, and accommodations. Opting to stay in Seminyak means indulging in luxury villas and impeccably designed hotels.

A favorite among both expatriates and tourists with discerning tastes, Seminyak boasts Instagram-worthy cafes, restaurants adorned with awe-inspiring interiors, and rejuvenating spas offering a range of treatments from manicures to massages.

The coastline is dominated by the renowned Double Six Beach, where visitors can rent umbrellas, settle into beanbags, and soak in the ambiance while Balearic beats fill the air from the numerous beachside restaurants and bars.

Where To Stay In Seminyak

W Bali is a haven of opulent luxury, ensuring your Bali experience remains etched in your memory. This exceptional 5-star hotel is nestled within an expansive complex, featuring a stunning pool area adjacent to Seminyak Beach, a restaurant offering a diverse culinary selection, and a late-night cocktail bar. The rooms epitomize spaciousness and modernity, characterized by sleek interiors and outdoor terraces. For those seeking more privacy, the private villas boast personal pools. Moreover, this prime location allows convenient access to all of Seminyak's trendy eateries and bars.

The Haven Bali lives up to its name with its decor adorned in light, neutral tones, soft greys, and natural wood, offering tasteful and comfortable accommodations. Among these stylish rooms, some feature private kitchens, lounges, and personal pools, adding an extra touch of "living the dream." The resort boasts a sophisticated shared pool for guests to enjoy, alongside an on-site spa to unwind in. At this 4-star haven, the restaurant presents a menu of organic delights, while the bar serves beverages and delectable Italian cuisine. Conveniently located nearby are Seminyak Square shopping mall and Legian Art Market.

Grandmas Plus Hotel stands out as a contemporary and trendy destination, characterized by minimalist interiors punctuated with playful colors and captivating artwork. The atmosphere is lively, with a vibrant bar area hosting live music performances in the evenings. For those seeking relaxation during the day, the hotel offers an outdoor pool and a spa. The on-site restaurant serves delectable cuisine alongside sunset cocktails. Cultural activities such as yoga and cooking classes are also available for guests to partake in. Moreover, this enjoyable stay places you mere moments away from the renowned Seminyak Beach.

KUTA

To experience a unique blend of relaxed coastal vibes and a lively urban atmosphere, Kuta is the ideal choice. As one of Bali's initial tourist hubs, Kuta offers an array of amenities to suit every preference.

Kuta has it all, ranging from upscale restaurants to local eateries, and private villas to budget-friendly accommodations. Additionally, the area is a shopper's delight, offering the opportunity to acquire your piece of Balinese design.

Known for its consistent waves, Kuta is a prime destination for surfing, catering to both pros and newcomers. Even if you're a beginner, numerous places provide board rentals and lessons, allowing you to give surfing a shot.

For vibrant nightlife, the nearby district of Legian is just a short walk from Kuta, ensuring a bustling and lively evening scene.

Where To Stay In Kuta

The Patra Bali Resort – Located right on the sands of South Kuta Beach, this upscale resort features an expansive lagoon pool and a coffee shop offering delicious meals. The property boasts tennis courts and sprawls across lush, grassy grounds adorned with abundant greenery. The rooms come in various sizes and configurations, each spacious and adorned with dark wood furnishings. Balconies open up to tropical vistas. The resort includes a kids club and a variety of activities to enjoy, such as water polo and cooking lessons.

Amnaya Resort Kuta – The generously sized rooms at the Amnaya Resort are adorned with subtle accents, polished tiled floors, plush furniture, and large beds. Floor-to-ceiling windows flood the rooms with natural light, all within a sleek yet rustic design. The resort features a serene outdoor pool and a hotel restaurant offering an extensive range of breakfast options as well as evening meals. Conveniently located near Discovery Shopping Mall and Waterbom Bali, there's no shortage of activities to enjoy right at your doorstep.

Cara Cara Inn – Offering a blend of fun and funkiness, Cara Cara Inn is a chic hostel that finds its home within a stunning Balinese villa. Guests can spend their days indulging in poolside delights, socializing in the hostel lounge, or basking in the sun on the rooftop terrace. The private rooms showcase polished concrete aesthetics, while the dormitories feature unique custom-made pod-style beds. An excellent choice for those on a budget while visiting Bali, this 3-star gem is conveniently located near Kuta Square and is just a short distance from Kuta Art Market – an ideal spot for souvenir shopping.

CANGGU

North of Seminyak lies the laid-back yet stylish enclave of Canggu. This area is peppered with wholefood cafes, trendy bars, and colorful beachside establishments that effortlessly invite you to spend a day by the ocean in this creatively vibrant slice of Bali.

Canggu, like many parts of Bali, offers an excellent surfing experience. Its beaches provide the perfect setting for riding the waves, with some featuring distinctive black sand. Along the northern coastline, you'll discover the enchanting Tanah Lot, a Balinese temple set on a rocky island amidst the sea.

Staying in Canggu doesn't require breaking the bank, thanks to a range of affordable yet chic hotels. For those willing to spend a bit more, there are also more luxurious options available in this picturesque area.

Where To Stay In Canggu

The Haven Suites – Blending contemporary minimalism with traditional Balinese charm, every room at The Haven Suites showcases wood accents, high ceilings, intricate tiled floors, and inviting ambient lighting. The hotel's design takes a prominent role, characterized by large glass windows, exposed brick, and concrete elements. The property boasts a spacious outdoor pool, as well as a separate pool for children. Guests can savor meals at the hotel's restaurant, or opt to rent a bike and explore the various nearby dining options. Alternatively, you can head to Berawa Beach right next door for surfing or simply basking in the sun.

SANUR

Sanur's unique ability to strike a balance between being a resort town and retaining its laid-back, authentic charm is the key to its immense popularity. Nestled on the southeastern side of the island, beyond Denpasar, it offers a distinct ambiance – more refined and tranquil compared to the lively west side of the isthmus.

Sanur boasts an abundance of large hotels, making it an excellent choice for family getaways. Its proximity to the airport adds to the convenience factor. The town's mature and relaxed atmosphere provides ample opportunities for enjoyment: a sandy beach adorned with traditional fishing boats, a scenic coastal cycling path, and tree-lined avenues dotted with quality shops and restaurants.

A highlight in Sanur is the magnificent Blanjong Temple, masterfully crafted from coral. The temple also boasts 10th-century inscriptions of historical significance to Bali, along with charming lotus ponds.

Where To Stay In Sanur

Puri Santrian – Nestled right on the shores of Sanur Beach, a stay here is a luxurious experience of lounging on palm-fringed sunbeds with a mesmerizing sea view. The rooms at Puri Santrian embody elegance and tradition, featuring rattan furnishings juxtaposed with crisp linens and gleaming, tiled floors. The entire resort exudes beauty. Multiple pools offer relaxation while indulging in luxury Balinese massages adds to the pampering. With two restaurants, yoga classes, a library, and more, there's no shortage of amenities. Notably, Denpasar is a mere 15-minute drive away from this budget-friendly paradise.

Peneeda View Beach Hotel – At Peneeda View Beach Hotel, you have the choice of staying in a cottage, bungalow, or spacious family suite, all tailored to your preferences. The hotel's decor seamlessly blends dark wood and simple style with traditional elements. An on-site restaurant serves local Balinese cuisine, while evenings are enhanced with live entertainment at the bar. During the day, you can stroll along Sanur Beach or take a refreshing dip in any of the four outdoor pools available for your enjoyment.

JIMBARAN

Situated south of Bali's airport and away from the bustling city scene of Kuta, Jimbaran on the Bukit Peninsula offers a tranquil beach retreat. This destination maintains its fishing village ambiance, featuring several beaches, striking cliffs, and an array of delectable seafood restaurants.

Despite its charming village atmosphere, Jimbaran offers a selection of luxurious hotels. This makes sense given its proximity to the airport and its serene setting away from the bustling southeastern action of Kuta and Legian.

Surfing takes center stage in Jimbaran. The expansive crescent of white sand provides ideal conditions for those eager to try their hand at catching waves. Alternatively, lounging on the beach and immersing yourself in the paradisiacal vibes of Jimbaran is a perfect way to spend your time.

Where To Stay In Jimbaran

Keraton Jimbaran Resort – A world of experiences awaits you at this upscale resort, including romantic candlelit beachside dinners, refreshing swims in the outdoor pool, and lively beach volleyball games. With three distinct on-site restaurants, you'll always have a variety of culinary choices. While a communal pool is available, the highlight is the private villas, each featuring its secluded pool. The essence of Keraton Jimbaran Resort lies in its rustic and intricately carved wooden furniture, adorning light and airy rooms with contemporary bathrooms. Each accommodation also offers a private balcony or terrace, adding to the allure of this enchanting destination.

ULUWATU

Uluwatu, situated well away from the bustling tourist districts of northern Bali, offers a refreshing escape on the Bukit Peninsula. The range of hotels in Uluwatu perfectly complements its atmosphere, spanning from relaxed options to upscale cliffside retreats adorned with Balinese aesthetics and luxury features like infinity pools.

A stay in Uluwatu places you conveniently close to the airport, yet far enough away to provide a true sense of relaxation and a getaway.

On the extreme southwest of the peninsula lies the remarkable Uluwatu Temple, a captivating clifftop religious site where you can witness the enigmatic kecak dance and be captivated by breathtaking sunsets.

Where To Stay In Uluwatu:

Suarga Padang Padang – Beyond its beautifully rustic beach-hut style and spacious tiled rooms, Suarga Padang Padang stands out for its breathtaking views. Perched high on the cliffs, this 5-star gem offers stunning sea vistas. The hotel seamlessly blends with the natural surroundings, constructed mainly from recycled wood and bamboo. Guests can swim in outdoor pools, surf at Padang Padang Beach, or use the hotel bicycles to reach the awe-inspiring Uluwatu Temple.

PinkCoco Bali – PinkCoco Bali exudes a charming kitschiness, featuring rooms. with whitewashed walls, polished concrete floors, and delightful splashes of vibrant pink. Some rooms at this 3-star haven boast private balconies, providing a tranquil space to unwind. A mere five-minute walk from Padang Padang Beach, it offers a relaxing environment with three outdoor pools surrounded by sun loungers. The on-site restaurant serves a fusion of Italian cuisine and sushi.

LEGIAN

Located a short distance north of Kuta's bustling tourist center, Legian is the ultimate destination for party enthusiasts. Jalan Legian buzzes with bars and clubs, and the beachfront location offers a perfect place to relax after a night of revelry.

Opting to stay in Legian positions you in the heart of the action. Accommodations range from beachfront properties to inland apartments and villas. For a touch of luxury, there are also upscale options available.

Legian is a shopping haven, providing numerous opportunities to find great deals. As the sun sets, unwind with a famous Bali sundowner on the beach before exploring the lively nightlife of Legian's vibrant drinking establishments.

Where To Stay In Legian

Pullman Bali Legian Beach – Nestled on Kuta Beach, this stylish hotel offers a luxurious retreat. With all the amenities expected from a 5-star establishment, including two lagoon pools, a rooftop infinity pool, three bars, a restaurant, a superb spa, and a fitness center, the Pullman tempts guests to stay in. Both Legian Art Market and Beachwalk Shopping Mall are within walking distance. Rooms feature tasteful simplicity, incorporating dark wood floors, spacious beds, and expansive bathrooms with captivating beach views.

The Akmani Legian – A mere five-minute walk from Kuta Beach, The Akmani Legian is ensconced amidst lush vegetation and tropical blooms. This 4-star gem boasts a rooftop bar and lounge for sunset cocktails, along with a restaurant offering diverse cuisine options. The rooms feature a serene color palette and subtle wooden accents. The vibrant nightlife and daytime shopping are just steps away, including attractions like Legian Art Market and Hard Rock Cafe.

NUSA LEMBONGAN

Situated off the coastline of the larger Nusa Penida and in proximity to the smaller Nusa Ceningan, the renowned Nusa Lembongan feels like a serene escape from the lively pace of the Balinese mainland.

Once primarily frequented by laid-back surfers, this island is progressively evolving into one of Bali's favored getaways. Whether you're on a tight budget or seeking more luxurious options, you'll find an array of accommodations to suit your needs.

Exploring the island at your own pace is a highlight, as well-maintained paths meander across this picturesque landscape. Nusa Lembongan boasts stunning beaches, turquoise waters, glimpses of local life, and breathtaking coastal vistas, all a mere 30-minute boat ride from Bali.

Where To Stay In Nusa Lembongan

The Palm Grove Villas – Embracing a fusion of modern decor and traditional wooden elements with vibrant accents and minimalist design, The Palm Grove Villas offer a serene atmosphere. Nestled within lush, green gardens, this tranquil oasis features two outdoor swimming pools, a spa, and a fitness center for relaxation and exercise. The charming resort restaurant serves a variety of dishes throughout the day. With bicycle rental available, you can easily explore the surroundings. Close by, Mushroom Beach and its array of dining options are just steps away.

Koji Garden Huts – Offering traditional Balinese bungalows with thatched roofs, Koji Garden Huts presents an opportunity to experience authentic local accommodation. The huts feature modern, tiled bathrooms with the unique addition of outdoor rain showers. Each room boasts a veranda overlooking the garden, and an outdoor swimming pool provides a refreshing escape from the heat. Positioned right on Tamarind Beach, this 3-star gem is an ideal choice for beach enthusiasts, while also being conveniently near Mushroom Beach.

NUSA DUA

Located on the eastern side of Bali's Bukit Peninsula, Nusa Dua is a haven of opulent 5-star resorts, an 18-hole golf course, and expansive pristine beaches for ultimate relaxation. With calm seas, the focus here shifts from surfing to gentle paddling and swimming.

Beyond Geger Beach lies Geger Temple, an attraction that provides insights into Balinese culture. The intricate carvings on the rocky outcrop, surrounded by the sea, exude an ancient and almost mystical ambiance.

Heading north, you'll reach the peninsula of Tanjung Benoa, which offers more budget-friendly accommodations, and the village of Benoa itself. The area has seen significant development and offers various activities, including watersports, to cater to the influx of visitors.

Where To Stay In Nusa Dua

INAYA Putri Bali – A sleek and sophisticated upscale hotel, INAYA Putri Bali offers ultimate comfort and relaxation. The rooms seamlessly blend Balinese aesthetics with contemporary design. Within its 9.1 hectares of lush grounds, you'll find numerous outdoor pools, three restaurants, a cocktail lounge, and a beach bar. Perfect for couples and families seeking a luxurious 5-star option on the beach, INAYA Putri Bali is located along the seafront in Nusa Dua, with additional beaches to explore in the vicinity.

Ayodya Resort Bali – Another upscale luxury gem, Ayodya Resort Bali stretches across 300 meters of private beach and boasts an expansive outdoor pool nestled in immaculate gardens. The architecture reflects the traditional Balinese style, echoed in the interiors. The spacious rooms feature large beds, parquet floors, and intricate wooden accents. Dining areas blend classic modernism with Balinese aesthetics, creating a grand and exotic ambiance. The hotel is conveniently close to the Bali Collection Shopping Centre, less than a kilometer away.

AMED

For travelers seeking an authentic Bali experience, Amed is an excellent choice. Consisting of a group of fishing villages along East Bali's northern coast, Amed exudes a genuine and traditional charm that remains unaffected by the influx of tourists.

Accommodation in Amed is budget-friendly and appealing to backpackers, as the area has yet to experience the heavy tourist presence found elsewhere. The roads were paved only as recently as 2000, and while some development and hotels have emerged in Candidasa, Amed's quiet allure endures. Travelers to Amed can enjoy superb scuba diving opportunities and find serenity through yoga sessions.

Visiting Amed offers the chance to appreciate its unspoiled atmosphere before it potentially evolves into a hub of boutiques and trendy cafes. The distant views of Mount Agung add to the area's natural beauty.

Where To Stay In Amed

Oasis – An economical option for Bali travelers, the Oasis, managed by a French team, is nestled within tropical gardens and features an outdoor swimming pool. The rooms are simple yet contemporary, adorned with white tiled floors, clean linens, and rustic stone-clad bathrooms. A delectable daily breakfast is provided. This 3-star lodging is conveniently positioned across from Amed Beach, and the Amed Ferry Terminal is also near.

NUSA PENIDA

Nusa Penida, a small island off Bali's southeastern coast, offers a tranquil escape within an escape. This pristine island serves as a glimpse into Bali's past, before the influx of tourists, showcasing unspoiled natural beauty and a paradise-like environment.

The island's hilly terrain is ideal for hiking, providing excellent trails and breathtaking cliffside vistas that reward adventurous hikers with expansive sea views. Nusa Penida's coastline is a treasure trove of hidden coves and vivid turquoise lagoons, inviting exploration. The nearby islands of Nusa Lembongan and Nusa Ceningan are easily accessible for further discovery.

Accommodation in Nusa Penida is readily available, primarily in the northern region, and includes budget-friendly options such as hotels, homestays, and bungalows, often infused with charming Balinese architectural elements.

Where To Stay In Nusa Penida

Coco Resort Penida – Coco Resort Penida offers elegantly designed bungalows that feature rattan walls, traditional hardwood furnishings, comfortable low beds, and terraces overlooking the garden or swimming pool. Guests can indulge in Balinese spa treatments and massages, and the resort provides an open-air restaurant and bar. Situated just a three-minute drive from Crystal Bay Beach, the resort offers bike and car rental services for guests' convenience.

Chapter 5: Places To Visit

Indonesia's vast array of islands includes Bali, an undisputed favorite known for being the quintessential tropical paradise. With its captivating scenery, vibrant culture, and spiritual atmosphere, Bali has become a top choice for travelers in search of an unforgettable journey. This idyllic tropical destination seamlessly combines pristine beaches, lush rice terraces, enchanting temples, and warm hospitality, resulting in a mosaic of marvels that deeply resonate.

Referred to as the Island of the Gods, Bali's culture is heavily influenced by a unique form of Hinduism that permeates all aspects of Balinese life. This is evident in the abundance of temples that grace every corner of the island and the daily rituals practiced in every household.

Despite some parts of Bali succumbing to excessive commercialization in recent times, there remain pockets of the island that remain unspoiled by the passage of time. Whether immersing oneself in the distinct Balinese culture, exploring vibrant coral reefs through scuba diving, conquering ancient volcanoes, or basking on expansive beaches, Bali ensures that it offers a slice of paradise for every single visitor.

Canggu

Situated on the southwestern coast of Bali, Canggu is a rapidly developing destination that offers a laid-back atmosphere with modern attractions. It is renowned for its picturesque rice fields, stunning beaches, and vibrant surf culture, making it a popular destination for surfers, digital nomads, and travelers seeking a more relaxed and bohemian vibe.

The area is home to a variety of trendy cafes, stylish boutiques, and beach clubs, creating a lively social atmosphere, especially in the evenings. Tourists can visit the renowned Echo Beach, renowned for its excellent surf breaks and beautiful sunsets, or venture inland to explore tranquil rice terraces and traditional Balinese villages.

For those looking for relaxation and self-care, Canggu also offers a top-tier wellness scene, with numerous yoga studios and retreats.

Nusa Penida

Nestled along Bali's southeastern coast, Nusa Penida is a haven of rugged beauty and untouched scenery.

Renowned for its awe-inspiring cliffs, shimmering turquoise waters, and immaculate white sand beaches, Nusa Penida provides a serene retreat from the busy mainland.

The striking coastal features of Nusa Penida, such as the iconic Kelingking Beach and Broken

Beach, leave visitors marveling at the artistic wonders of nature. Snorkeling and diving enthusiasts will be enchanted by the vibrant marine life that thrives in areas like Crystal Bay and Manta Point.

Simultaneously, travelers who venture into the heart of the island will discover lush jungles, cascading waterfalls, and traditional villages where they can immerse themselves in the local way of life.

While the infrastructure may not be as developed as Bali's main tourist hubs, the unrefined beauty, and spirit of exploration render Nusa Penida a destination of utmost importance for those seeking unique and off-the-beaten-path adventures.

Sekumpul Waterfall

Bali is home to numerous remarkable waterfalls, and Sekumpul Waterfall is among the most awe-inspiring.

Located in the highlands of Bali's northern region, it captivates visitors with its forceful cascades and verdant surroundings. The journey requires trekking through dense forests, crossing streams, and traversing rocky terrain. However, the reward is the breathtaking view of multiple towering waterfalls descending into a tranquil pool below, leaving a lasting impression.

The immense size and magnificence of the falls create a captivating display, enhanced by the misty ambiance that enhances the enchantment. Nature enthusiasts and photographers will find themselves fully immersed in the tranquility and majestic beauty of this natural wonder.

Jimbaran

Situated along Bali's southwestern coast, Jimbaran is a captivating coastal village that seamlessly blends traditional allure with contemporary opulence. Most renowned for its unspoiled beaches and breathtaking sunsets, Jimbaran provides a tranquil and unhurried atmosphere perfect for both relaxation and exploration.

The crescent-shaped Jimbaran Bay, stretching for 3 kilometers, is adorned with golden sands and swaying palm trees, creating an idyllic backdrop for unwinding and enjoying beachside dining. Seafood enthusiasts can savor a delectable spread of freshly grilled seafood at local beachfront eateries.

Luxury resorts and spas are also prominent in Jimbaran, offering world-class amenities and revitalizing treatments that promise relaxation and stress relief.

For those with an interest in cultural immersion, the nearby Uluwatu Temple is an essential stop. Perched atop a cliff and commanding breathtaking views of the Indian Ocean, the temple offers a captivating glimpse into Bali's rich cultural heritage.

Surfers seeking exceptional swells should make their way to Balangan Beach and Dreamland Beach for an outstanding surfing experience.

Sidemen Valley

Bali isn't solely defined by its beaches, spa resorts, and vibrant nightlife; it also boasts lush countryside. The Sidemen Valley stands as a prime example of this.

Nestled in the eastern part of the island, this tranquil valley showcases stunning landscapes, terraced rice fields, and traditional Balinese villages.

For nature enthusiasts, it's a paradise offering scenic hikes, cycling tours, and leisurely countryside strolls. Accommodation options are abundant, ranging from boutique resorts to homestays, providing a chance to fully engage in local culture and embrace Balinese warmth.

Exploring Sidemen unveils an authentic Balinese existence, with artisans crafting intricate handicrafts and locals tending their rice fields. The valley's beauty and serenity create an ideal setting for those seeking a peaceful retreat and a closer bond with nature and Balinese customs.

West Bali National Park

Located at the western tip of Bali, the West Bali National Park stands as the island's sole national park, a pristine and ecologically diverse nature reserve that showcases Bali's innate marvels.

This expansive park encompasses lush rainforests, thriving mangrove forests, expansive savannahs, and vibrant coral reefs. Within its bounds reside numerous species of flora and fauna, among them endangered creatures such as the Bali Starling and Javan Rusa deer.

A paradise for nature enthusiasts and wildlife admirers, the park invites visitors to partake in guided treks, engaging bird-watching excursions, and immersive experiences. Through snorkeling or diving in the park's lively marine ecosystems, they can also explore the captivating underwater realm.

The park's renowned Pemuteran Bay is a favored diving location and serves as a hub for turtle conservation. Slightly off the northeast shore of the peninsula, Menjangan Island awaits, offering historical Hindu temples, indigenous barking deer, and breathtaking coral reefs.

Bedugul

If you're finding the tropical heat of Bali overwhelming, consider a visit to Bedugul. Nestled in the central highlands, this picturesque retreat offers a welcome respite from the intense sun.

This charming mountain town is celebrated for its cooler climate and stunning natural vistas. Imagine tranquil lakes, verdant forests, and mist-kissed landscapes that are sure to leave you in awe.

Don't miss the iconic Ulun Danu Beratan Temple, positioned on Lake Beratan's shores. Its intricate Balinese architecture and reflections on the water create captivating photo opportunities.

Bedugul is also home to the Bali Botanic Garden, a haven for plant enthusiasts, and the Bali Treetop Adventure Park, where thrilling treetop obstacle courses await amidst the forest canopy. Additionally, the region is renowned for its fresh produce, offering farm-to-table dining experiences and vibrant local markets for visitors to enjoy.

Jatiluwih

Bali is renowned for its captivating rice terraces, and Jatiluwih stands out as one of the prime locations to witness their splendor.

Offering a captivating insight into the island's agricultural heritage, Jatiluwih boasts expansive terraced fields that gracefully descend the undulating hills, forming a breathtaking tableau of vibrant green shades.

The region is celebrated for its traditional Subak irrigation system, a method that has nurtured rice cultivation for centuries. Travelers can explore these terraces on foot or rent bicycles to fully immerse themselves in the tranquil countryside.

During these journeys, interactions with local farmers and glimpses of traditional Balinese village life are common occurrences. Jatiluwih also presents panoramic viewpoints like the Pura Luhur Batukaru Temple, offering visitors a chance to revel in the majestic landscapes.

If possible, aim to visit Jatiluwih at dusk when the setting sun casts its enchanting hues upon the landscape, creating a magical glow that's perfect for capturing Insta-worthy moments.

Nusa Dua

Nestled along Bali's southern coast, Nusa Dua is a renowned destination for luxury resorts, providing travelers with a sophisticated and indulgent experience.

Famed for its pristine beaches, crystal-clear waters, and high-end resorts, Nusa Dua exudes a refined and tranquil atmosphere. The area is home to a variety of opulent hotels, stylish villas, and upscale restaurants, catering to those seeking a combination of comfort and relaxation.

Nusa Dua's palm-lined beaches make for a perfect setting for sunbathing, swimming, and participating in water sports. Golfers will find joy at the renowned Bali National Golf Club.

For those interested in culture, the nearby Pasifika Museum is a must-see, featuring an extensive art collection from across the Asia-Pacific region. Nusa Dua is also renowned for its water-blow phenomenon, where the crashing waves create dramatic water sprays.

When planning a visit to Nusa Dua, it is important to note that it is an upscale part of Bali, resulting in higher prices compared to other areas of the island.

Pura Lempuyang

The renowned Pura Lempuyang, also known as the 'Gateway to Heaven', is a sacred Hindu temple complex situated on the slopes of Mount Lempuyang in East Bali, at an elevation of 600 meters. It has gained international recognition for its breathtaking views and profound spiritual significance. The most remarkable feature of the complex is its iconic split-gate entrance, which offers a stunning view of Mount Agung, the highest volcano in Bali.

To reach the summit, visitors must climb a long staircase with various temples, a journey that has a deep spiritual meaning for many. The temple complex exudes a peaceful atmosphere, inviting people to connect with their spirituality and experience Balinese Hindu culture.

Witnessing the temple bathed in a golden hue during sunrise is a truly remarkable experience, one that is worth getting up early for.

Tukad Cepung Waterfall

For an awe-inspiring waterfall experience, Tukad Cepung Waterfall is a must-see destination.

Located within a cave in Tembuku village, which is part of the Bangli regency on the island, this enchanting site is situated approximately 30 km away from Ubud.

To reach the waterfall, a brief hike through lush greenery and narrow pathways is required. Upon arrival, you'll be greeted by a towering cliff that encircles the waterfall, creating a distinctive and picturesque scene.

The waterfall gracefully descends into a shallow pool, tempting visitors to indulge in its crystalline waters. Natural rock formations surrounding the waterfall enhance its allure and offer excellent opportunities for capturing photos.

As sunlight filters through the narrow canyon, it bathes the cascading water in a mesmerizing glow, resulting in a truly magical experience.

Visitors have the chance to unwind, meditate, or simply absorb the natural beauty of the surroundings. For the best experience, aim to visit between 9 a.m. and 11 a.m. when the waterfall is showcased in its finest light.

Mount Agung

Exploring Mount Agung is indeed an exciting and rewarding adventure for both nature enthusiasts and adventurers. The hike up this active volcano leads through a diverse range of terrains, including lush forests, rugged trails, and volcanic ash fields. The ultimate reward is the breathtaking panoramic views of the island and its surroundings that hikers can enjoy from the summit.

The spiritual significance of Mount Agung holds a special place in the hearts of the Balinese people. The presence of the Besakih Temple, often referred to as the 'Mother Temple of Bali', at the volcano's base adds to the reverence. This temple allows visitors to participate in traditional ceremonies and immerse themselves in Bali's dynamic cultural heritage.

While conquering Mount Agung demands physical strength and endurance, the experience is unparalleled. It forges a deep bond with nature and offers insights into Bali's spiritual customs.

Those who set out early are treated to the extraordinary spectacle of a sunrise from the summit, a moment that remains etched in memory forever.

Sanur Beach

Situated in Denpasar village in southeast Bali, the tranquil Sanur Beach has gained popularity among older visitors, earning it the playful moniker "Snore Beach." However, this nickname doesn't accurately reflect the range of activities available at this coastal resort.

Beyond its pristine beach, Sanur boasts several significant historical sites. The Blanjong Temple, home to inscriptions dating back to the 9th century, stands as a testament to the area's cultural heritage. Nearby, the Le Mayeur Museum was once the residence of Belgian impressionist Adrian Jean Le Mayeur and showcases his artwork.

Tourists can also venture into the nearby mangrove forest or embark on boat trips to the neighboring islands, offering a refreshing change of scenery and experiences.

Nusa Lembongan

Nusa Lembongan, a small island off Bali's southeast coast, stands as a tropical haven that beckons with its unspoiled beaches, turquoise waters, and laid-back island ambiance. A short boat ride away, it offers a serene escape from the bustling parts of Bali.

This island is celebrated for its captivating coastal landscapes, featuring highlights like Dream Beach, Mushroom Bay, and Devil's Tear, where powerful waves crash against rugged cliffs. Snorkeling and diving enthusiasts are in for a treat, as Nusa Lembongan boasts vibrant coral reefs and a rich array of marine life.

Exploring the island on a bicycle or scooter unveils picturesque scenes of lush jungles, quaint villages, and seaweed farms. Visitors can relish beachside dining, especially savoring fresh seafood, and bask in the beauty of breathtaking sunsets.

Lovina

Nestled on the northern coast of Bali, Lovina is a charming coastal town renowned for its tranquil beaches, dolphin-watching tours, and vibrant coral reefs. It is a place of relaxation and leisure, with its black sand beaches providing the perfect backdrop for sunbathing, swimming, and leisurely walks along the shore.

The town is particularly famous for its early morning dolphin-watching tours, which offer the chance to observe playful dolphin pods in their natural habitat. Snorkelers and divers will be enthralled by the vibrant underwater world, with its tropical fish and stunning coral formations.

Accommodation in Lovina ranges from budget-friendly guesthouses to luxurious resorts. Beyond the beaches, visitors can explore nearby attractions such as the Banjar Hot Springs and the Brahma Vihara Arama, a historic Buddhist temple.

Pura Luhur Uluwatu

Pura Luhur Uluwatu is a majestic temple in Bali that sits atop a cliff overlooking the Indian Ocean. It is a sacred temple that is famous for its picturesque sunsets and traditional Balinese architecture.

The temple is one of the six most important temples in Bali, believed to be the spiritual pillar of the island. It exudes a sense of ancient spirituality and serenity. Visitors can explore the temple complex, which is adorned with intricate stone carvings and guarded by mischievous resident monkeys.

The Kecak fire dance, performed against the backdrop of the setting sun, is a mesmerizing cultural experience. The temple's cliffside location also provides panoramic views of the ocean and rugged coastline, making it an ideal spot for photography and contemplation.

Mount Batur

Climbing Mount Batur is a popular activity for those with an adventurous spirit. This 1,717-meter (5,633-foot) peak is an active volcano with four craters, a lake, and several villages, and is situated in one of the most picturesque areas of Bali. The trek to the summit begins in the early morning and takes two to three hours, passing through volcanic landscapes and unique flora. As the sun rises, the sky changes to a range of colors, making the sunrise from the summit an unforgettable experience. After descending, visitors can relax in the hot springs at the volcano's base, and take in the stunning views of Lake Batur.

Kuta Beach

Once a tranquil fishing village, Kuta gained recognition as a great surfing spot in the 1970s and has since been Bali's top tourist destination. Located in the village of Kelurahan, the long, wide stretch of sand is one of the most beautiful and well-maintained beaches on the island.

The southern part of the beach is usually crowded, day or night, due to its lively nightlife. However, a short walk to the north end of the beach provides visitors with a peaceful atmosphere.

The beach is full of restaurants, bars, and shops, making it a bustling area. Visitors can savor local delicacies, shop for souvenirs, or enjoy the vibrant nightlife with beachfront clubs and live music venues, many of which stay open until the early hours of the morning.

Pura Besakih

Nestled on the slopes of Gunung Agung, Bali's highest mountain, Pura Besakih is considered the most important of the nine directional temples that were built to protect the island from negative forces. This temple was named after the dragon god that is believed to live in the depths of the mountain. The temple complex is made up of more than 28 structures that are situated on seven ascending terraces.

Pura Besakih is a sacred destination for the Balinese, often hosting colorful ceremonies and religious festivals.

It is a great opportunity for travelers to observe the island's ancient spiritual customs, which have been around for thousands of years. Visitors can explore the intricate architecture, stone carvings, and beautiful pagodas that are found on the temple grounds. The stunning views of the surrounding mountains and valleys add to the amazing experience. It is recommended to take part in an organized tour to view the site, as the self-appointed guides on site can be quite insistent.

Seminyak

Nestled along the southwestern shoreline of Bali, Seminyak emerges as a quaint coastal town that finds itself embraced by the burgeoning urban expanse of Kuta. However, despite its proximity to the energetic hub of Kuta, Seminyak has carved out a distinct niche as one of the most coveted havens for holidaymakers on the island. Its allure extends a magnetic pull for discerning globetrotters of means, drawn by an array of opulent offerings. From its array of high-end boutiques showcasing the latest trends to its constellation of five-star gastronomic experiences, sumptuous hotels that redefine luxury, and lavish spas that pamper the senses, Seminyak casts an irresistible spell that attracts a global elite.

Yet, it's not just the promise of material indulgence that beckons visitors to its embrace.

Seminyak Beach, while rendering its waves too robust for leisurely swims, serves up a feast for the eyes with its sweeping views of the boundless Indian Ocean. Here, the horizon dances with the silhouettes of skilled surfers who flock to challenge the formidable waves, creating an entrancing spectacle that captivates both enthusiasts and onlookers.

As twilight blankets the scenery, Seminyak metamorphoses into a pulsating hub of nocturnal fervor. The town throbs with life as its vivacious nightlife springs to life. Along the waterfront, a symphony of beachfront bars and clubs awakens, casting a bewitching ambiance that invites revelers to lose themselves in the rhythm of the night. Here, under the moon's gentle glow, you can surrender to the music's embrace and dance the hours away, weaving unforgettable memories into the very fabric of Seminyak's vibrant tapestry.

Tanah Lot

Situated gracefully upon a massive rocky outcrop, Tanah Lot stands as an eminent Hindu temple, casting an enduring spell of fame across the enchanting landscape of Bali. With roots that stretch deep into the annals of Balinese mythology, this temple emerges as one of the crown jewels among the seven sea temples that adorn the southwestern fringes of Bali. Strategically positioned in an interconnected formation, these temples offer a breathtaking maritime panorama that pays homage to both spirituality and nature's splendor.

Earning its rightful place as a pinnacle of Bali's tourist attractions, Tanah Lot attracts a throng of seekers, drawn to its magnetic aura from both local realms and distant shores. The ebb and flow of visitors reach their crescendo during the waning hours of the day, as the sun's golden rays paint the sky, setting the stage for an awe-inspiring sunset spectacle. In this vibrant arena, where land and sea embrace, an animated tapestry unfolds—shops brimming with treasures beckon, a bustling market exudes life, and the air buzzes with anticipation.

Venturing forth from the lively market labyrinth onto the sun-kissed beach, a panorama of breathtaking proportions emerges—a resplendent temple poised with elegance upon its rocky pedestal, its silhouette an emblem of unwavering devotion amidst nature's grandeur. As the sun dips towards the horizon, a symphony of hues dances across the sky, casting a shimmering reflection upon the waters that cradle the temple's foundations. Here, where the terrestrial and the divine converge, an ethereal tableau is born, a harmonious blend of architectural marvel and untamed beauty.

The meeting of the temple's ancient stone and the vast expanse of the ocean creates a scene that transcends the ordinary, etching an indelible mark upon the canvas of memory. The tranquil devotion that shaped the temple's foundations finds its mirror in the rhythmic lapping of waves against the rock, an eternal duet that resonates with those who come to witness this remarkable vista. In the realm of Tanah Lot, spirituality and natural wonder unite, leaving an imprint that lingers long after the sun has set and the tides have shifted.

Ubud

Nestled serenely amidst the cascading tiers of rice fields that ascend the foothills of Bali's central mountains, Ubud stands as the pulsating cultural nucleus of the island. Revered as Bali's epicenter of culture, Ubud boasts an array of significant museums, none more notable than the Neka Art Museum, which houses an extensive collection of mesmerizing Balinese paintings. The city comes alive with daily dance and music performances that reverberate through its streets, resonating with the rhythm of its artistic soul. Every corner teems with art galleries and craft boutiques, inviting exploration and immersion into Bali's creative tapestry.

Ubud's allure as a cultural haven is long-established, but it witnessed a meteoric rise in tourist footfall following its cameo in the pages of the book and the frames of the film "Eat, Pray, Love." Yet, a sanctuary of tranquillity awaits just a short stroll or bike ride away, where one can retreat from the masses and commercialism, rekindling a connection with the essence of Ubud.

For those with an affinity for nature's embrace, the nearby Monkey Forest stands as a hallowed haven, inhabited by mischievous macaque monkeys. As Ubud's heart beats amidst gently undulating rice paddies, an immersive symphony of green unfurls, painting the landscape with vibrant life. These verdant surroundings also open doors to exploration—trekking paths wind through the countryside, offering a close communion with nature, while cycling trails invite adventure. Traditional villages, such as the renowned Tegalalang Rice Terrace, beckon travelers to bask in their time-honored charm.

And for those seeking reprieve from spirited escapades, Ubud's fame as a global wellness and yoga retreat destination is well-deserved. Here, amidst this cultural nucleus, one can embark on a transformative journey, nurturing mind, body, and spirit, and emerge revitalized and replenished from this oasis of holistic rejuvenation.

Chapter 6: Experiencing Balinese Culture

Bali, renowned for its captivating natural splendor, is often called 'the island of deities.' Its landscape boasts magnificent cliffs, captivating beaches, verdant rice terraces, and concealed waterfalls.

However, Bali's allure extends beyond its breathtaking nature; it possesses a distinctive history and culture. Gaining a deeper comprehension of this enchanting island will greatly enhance your Bali experience.

Hinduism predominantly shapes Bali, introduced by Indian traders in the 7th century. While the rest of Indonesia adopted Islam in the 16th century, Bali became a sanctuary for artists and intellectuals, firmly upholding its Hindu traditions.

Europe's first foreign visitors reached Bali in the late 17th century, lured by spices. By the late 18th century, Bali fell under Dutch rule and remained so until Indonesia regained independence after World War II.

In the 1970s, Bali saw an influx of Australian tourists following a surfing documentary filmed on its shores. The early 2000s brought devastating terrorist attacks that inflicted severe damage on the tourism sector.

However, within a few years, Bali reclaimed its position on travelers' wish lists.

Bali is immersed in its rich cultural heritage, evident in the multitude of temples and ornate decorations gracing hotel lobbies. The local culture is intricately woven into the everyday lives of the residents, who frequently don traditional attire, participate in ceremonies, and place daily offerings at every street corner.

Life in Bali revolves around the Saka calendar, dictating significant events, be it a dental appointment or a wedding. To avert misfortune, seeking counsel from a local priest to determine an auspicious day is a necessity for important life affairs.

Tourists have the opportunity to engage in a variety of activities that provide insight into the captivating Balinese culture. Here are a few examples.

1. A Spiritual Journey To Tirta Empul

Participate in a traditional water cleansing ceremony at Tirta Empul. Ubud, known as Bali's cultural hub, offers an excellent opportunity to immerse yourself in the island's vibrant heritage. Adding a cleansing ritual to your Ubud visit allows you to engage directly with local customs.

The water cleansing ritual holds immense significance in Balinese Hindu culture. Locals frequent places like Tirta Empul, especially during major celebrations, to purify their souls of negativity and gather inspiration for daily life. Tirta Empul's spring water is believed to possess healing properties. Legend tells of a king who converted to Hinduism after using the spring to heal his troops.

Even foreign tourists are welcome to partake in the ritual. Entry to Tirta Empul is around 50K IDR ($3.5), and visitors should have attire covering their shoulders and knees. The temple provides sarongs for those without appropriate clothing.

The ceremony unfolds at the main spring pool, where changing rooms and lockers are available. Traditional green robes can be rented for the purification process. Join the line, starting at the left sprout. At each sprout, make a prayer, wash your face thrice, and immerse your head in the cold spring water three times. Repeat this at every sprout except the last two, reserved for burials.

2. Learn to Cook local Balinese Dishes

Prepare yourself for an enriching Balinese cooking class! Incorporating a cooking lesson into your Bali itinerary is a fantastic way to immerse yourself in the local culture.

Balinese cuisine reflects a blend of influences from different parts of Indonesia, as well as China and India. Guided by Hindu beliefs, beef consumption is rare, while rice holds a central place in the diet. The significance of food extends to religion, where specific dishes are prepared and consumed during important festivals, and others are offered to the gods.

Traditionally, Balinese families would buy ingredients in the morning from local markets, have a mid-morning meal, and save leftovers for the evening.

You can experience traditional Balinese dishes at local eateries known as Warungs. These

Warungs often specialize in particular dishes like Nasi Campur. Small carts stationed along local roads sell traditional breakfasts and snacks.

For the ultimate experience, opt for cooking classes hosted by Balinese families. These classes typically begin with a visit to a local market, where you'll learn about tropical fruits, vegetables, and spices that are also used in traditional medicine.

Back at the family's home, you'll create a meal using traditional methods like wood-fired ovens. Throughout the process, your host will share insights into daily family life and customs. The experience concludes with everyone savoring a fresh, delectable meal together.

3. Embrace the Mesmerizing Uluwatu Kecak Dance

Witness the captivating Kecak performance at Uluwatu Temple, a mesmerizing display of Balinese culture. In this culture, dance serves as both an artistic expression and a profound religious connection with the gods. These dances often take place during temple festivities across the island.

Passed down through generations, the art of dance is taught to young children, allowing them to connect with their heritage. Before performing, dancers typically offer prayers and sacrifices to receive divine inspiration from the gods.

Tourists have the opportunity to learn Balinese dances in local villages or participate in events organized by larger resort-style hotels. The array of traditional dances each carries a unique story.

Legong, performed by young girls adorned in elegant attire and gold ornaments, incorporates intricate hand movements and facial expressions. Baris, a warrior's dance, symbolizes battle preparation, while the Barong and Kris dance narrates the conflict between good and evil.

Among Bali's mesmerizing performances, the Kecak dance stands out, especially when staged at the iconic Uluwatu Temple during sunset. Overlooking the Indian Ocean atop a dramatic cliff, Uluwatu provides an exquisite backdrop for this awe-inspiring show.

During the Kecak dance, a sizable ensemble of men and boys don traditional sarongs. Chanting fervently, they form a circle, their raised hands a dramatic sight as the sun descends. Often, a central flame adds to the spectacle after twilight.

The Kecak dance recounts the tale of Prince Rama's battle against an evil king, and his quest to rescue the abducted princess Shinta. Previously, Kecak was a trance dance utilized by men when praying for their ancestors' souls. Presently, a female-led group in Ubud also performs this remarkable dance.

4. Explore the Garuda Wisnu Kencana Cultural Park

For those seeking a deeper understanding of Balinese heritage, arts, and legendary tales, Garuda Park offers an outstanding day trip. This cultural haven is home to a colossal 120-meter-tall statue depicting the Hindu deity Wisnu atop the mythical Garuda eagle.

This monument stands as Bali's most prominent landmark and holds the distinction of being the world's tallest statue of its kind, even surpassing the stature of Christ the Redeemer!

Garuda, the national emblem of Indonesia, symbolizes the triumph of freedom from oppression, holding significant meaning for the Indonesian people.

Within Garuda Wisnu Park, an array of cultural showcases enables visitors to delve into the intricate tapestry of Balinese heritage. Spectators can enjoy performances encompassing dances from various parts of Indonesia, folklore presentations recounting tales from different historical epochs, and Rindik instrumental concerts.

Additional attractions include a children's cinema screening of animated renditions of Balinese legends, a museum, a restaurant, a sizable upper-body statue of Wisnu, and a serene lotus pond.

5. Participate in a Batik Workshop Experience

Batik, an ancient craft with its origins in Java, holds a rich history. The term "Batik" is derived from the Javanese word "tik," meaning "to dot."

The Batik technique entails applying hot wax to silk or cotton fabric before immersing it in dye. The wax acts as a barrier, forming intricate patterns. Designs can encompass a single layer of wax and color, or intricate compositions featuring multiple layers of both.

While this technique is practiced globally, including in Malaysia, China, and Japan, Indonesian Batik is widely regarded for its exceptional artistry.

Numerous workshops provide opportunities for visitors to grasp the fundamentals of Batik, often led by local artists in Ubud. Participants employ traditional tools and learn to adorn their fabric pieces, which they can carry home as a keepsake.

For culture enthusiasts visiting Bali, the realm of Batik crafting offers a captivating endeavor. Which of these alternative Bali experiences resonates with you?

Chapter 7: Adventure and Activities

Engage in exciting experiences during your Bali trip, especially if you prefer nature over hotels. Bali offers diverse landscapes like valleys, lakes, rapids, and traditional villages. Discover less-explored parts with activities such as rice field treks and climbing peaks to witness stunning sunrises. These adventures highlight Bali's natural beauty, away from the usual tourist spots.

1.Embark on a private full-day expedition to Trunyan Village, an ancient lakeside settlement nestled in Bali's landscapes. Immerse yourself in the village's historical significance and distinct traditions, including its unique burial ceremonies. Departed locals are ferried by boat to a dedicated burial area near a fragrant tree, renowned for neutralizing decomposition odors. This remarkable and somewhat eerie display presents an unparalleled adventure, spanning approximately 8.5 hours. Engage with Trunyan's cultural practices and delve into its heritage, crafting memories that will last a lifetime.

2. Embark on an exciting whitewater rafting journey on the Ayung River, located near Ubud. This river is home to Bali's longest and most thrilling rapids. As soon as you step onto your raft, you will be navigating through Grade 2 and Grade 3 rapids, working together with your fellow adventurers to paddle and steer. With the help of professional rafting guides and the necessary gear, you will be taken through a wild ride of swirling foamy vortexes, natural ramps, refreshing waterfalls, and unexpected drops – a true nature-themed rollercoaster. After the thrilling water ride, you can dry off and enjoy a delicious gourmet buffet lunch. This unforgettable adventure will take approximately 5 hours.

3. Discover a captivating adventure with the Antungan Village Rice Field Trek and Blangsinga Waterfall Tour. Combining

adventure and accessibility, this Bali excursion offers a guided market exploration, a nature trek, and a waterfall discovery all in one delightful day in central Bali. Set amidst the lush Blahbatuh village in Gianyar regency, the journey includes walks through the scenic rice paddies of Antungan, where you can take a refreshing break with a young coconut and savor a local lunch.

The following ascent along a narrow forest trail leads you to the mesmerizing Blangsinga waterfalls, offering a chance for a refreshing dip while taking in the stunning vistas. The tour also encompasses a visit to Kemenuh Butterfly Park, showcasing a glimpse of Bali's remarkable winged creatures. Set aside about 8 hours to fully immerse yourself in this enriching experience.

4. Experience a private Sunrise Volcano Hike complemented by a hot spring bath and Kopi Luwak coffee indulgence. Ascend Mount Batur to witness the enchanting sunrise over the

expansive caldera lake. At the summit, savor a distinctive breakfast of egg and banana cooked using the volcano's steam.

The descent takes you through local plantations, providing a glimpse of fresh produce and a tasting session featuring various coffee blends, including the renowned Kopi Luwak.

Afterward, unwind with a relaxing soak in a hot spring on the lake's western side, where the 40°C water offers a soothing escape to revive weary muscles. Allocate approximately 10 hours for this comprehensive and rejuvenating adventure.

5. Experience an immersive full-day tour that allows you to explore both the Jatiluwih Rice Terraces and Batukaru Mountain. The Jatiluwih Rice Terraces, often dubbed Bali's 'sea of green', offer a serene and revitalizing highland vista, showcasing some of the island's most breathtaking sights. This area harmoniously blends verdant plantations, rice paddies, and lush tropical forests that envelop Mount Batukaru.

The tour encompasses a visit to the ancient Batukaru Temple, nestled on the slopes of the mountain. This 8-hour expedition to Bali's western region promises an engaging journey, providing the chance to embrace the natural allure and cultural significance of the surroundings.

6. Discover the ancient civilization of Tenganan Pegringsingan village in East Bali, one of the island's oldest settlements. This village is famous for its unique tie-dye cloths called gringsing, which lend the village its name. Immerse yourself in this tour that provides a rare chance to explore the heritage site and witness the enduring ancient customs upheld by the villagers. Indulge in sampling local palm wine and appreciating the intricately crafted items. The journey concludes with a visit to the golden shores of Virgin Beach in the coastal village of Perasi. Allow approximately 8 hours to fully absorb this captivating experience.

7. For nature enthusiasts and thrill-seekers exploring Bali, engage in an exhilarating Quad or Buggy Driving Adventure combined with a Tubing Excursion. This high-energy experience unfolds in the scenic village of Payangan, nestled in the central highlands north of Ubud. Traverse the highland forest and plantation trails, either riding ATVs (quad bikes) or specially designed dirt buggies.

The excitement-filled journey culminates with a unique and refreshing activity – cruising down the Siap River rapids on large inflatable tubes. Complete with wetsuits, helmets, lifejackets, safety harnesses, and a delectable Balinese lunch, this thrilling adventure extends over approximately 7 hours. Enjoy the rush of the ride and the excitement of river exploration all in one unforgettable day.

8. Embark on the Wakaland 4x4 Island Tour, delving into Bali's rugged interior for a diverse array of sights including rice paddies, historic quarries, and lofty mountain summits. This

journey offers an authentic glimpse into the heart of Bali's central region and its breathtaking landscapes.

The adventure kicks off in the morning, starting with a visit to an ancient Balinese village boasting a sandstone quarry where skilled artisans carve life-sized masterpieces. Trek through lush rice fields, engage in crafting Balinese flower offerings known as canang sari and ascend into the mountains via the Jatiluwih rice fields. A lunch featuring Balinese delights and coffee is included in the excursion. Allocate around 8.5 hours to fully immerse yourself in this captivating tour.

9. Indulge in a concise yet enriching Hidden Rice Terraces Small-Group Tour, ideal for a taste of Bali's lush countryside. Situated near the popular resort regions of Kuta, Legian, and Seminyak, this tour offers an exploration of the green rice paddies in the Kerobokan area. Here, you'll discover vast expanses of lush farmland, providing an off-the-beaten-path encounter.

The guided trek through the rice fields unveils fascinating insights, featuring a visit to an eclectic warehouse brimming with unique antiques, as well as a stop at a local traditional market. Despite its brevity, this short tour of about 3 hours delivers a remarkable glimpse into the serene beauty and cultural treasures of Bali's countryside.

10. Embark on thrilling Fishing Boat Trips for captivating Bali marine adventures. These trips offer an enjoyable way to explore the island's stunning coastlines while experiencing a fresh perspective of its beauty. Numerous marine adventure and water sports companies in Bali provide fishing tours and charters, often paired with dive excursions.

Led by experienced boat captains and crews, these half-day cruises take you to picturesque locations, equipped with fishing rods, lures, and lines for an exciting fishing experience. Bali's coastal waters are abundant with big-game fish, making the journey itself an exhilarating part of the adventure. And, of course, the excitement culminates when you successfully reel in prized catches like mahi-mahi, wahoo, barracuda, or even blue marlin!

Chapter 8: Shopping and Souvenirs in Bali

Bali is a paradise for shopaholics, offering remarkable shopping opportunities that will delight visitors from all corners of the globe. From designer-label goods at unbeatable prices to an abundance of boutiques brimming with unique finds, the shopping scene here is a true haven. Immerse yourself in the local culture by exploring the myriad local shops, street markets, and shopping malls that await, promising an exhilarating shopping spree. Craft a shopping list of desired souvenirs and prepare to explore some of the finest shopping destinations Bali has to offer.

Best Shopping Destinations In Bali

Seeking a memorable souvenir or a thoughtful gift? Maybe a designer handbag or hand-painted artwork? Bali offers an array of captivating shopping experiences, ranging from iconic roadside stalls to upscale malls and sprawling beachfront bazaars. With favorable exchange rates, visitors from across the globe can indulge in incredible deals. Below, we explore the prime shopping destinations on the island.

1. Kuta Art Market

Nestled along the Kuta Beach boardwalk, the Kuta Art Market is a haven for dedicated shoppers, boasting an eclectic range of wares from canvas tote bags to straw hats. This beachfront outdoor market features an extensive selection, all sourced from local vendors. By shopping here, you're contributing to the local businesses in the area.

Comprising six spacious buildings divided into individual vendor stalls, the Kuta Art Market offers a diverse array of goods. It's an ideal spot to discover souvenirs and gifts to bring back home. Within the market, street food vendors also provide quick Indonesian bites for those exploring. With reasonable prices, bargaining-savvy visitors can secure excellent deals. The market operates daily from 8 a.m. to 10 p.m., offering a rewarding shopping experience by the sea.

2. Mal Bali Galeria

Mal Bali Galeria stands as a spacious urban hub, offering a one-stop destination for visitors in search of high-end fashion, accessories, electronics, and gifts, all available at reasonable prices. Regarded as one of the premier shopping malls globally, Mal Bali Galeria caters to those seeking the latest brands like Cartier, Calvin Klein, and Versace, among others, all conveniently housed under a single roof.

This mall presents a diverse array of offerings, including an Ace Hardware store and an array of dining options. Its open-air layout encompasses a sprawling food court serving delectable international fare. Whether you're craving Indonesian cuisine, Chinese dishes, or a classic

American-style burger, the food court has you covered. The weekends come alive with live entertainment such as music concerts, food and gadget demos, and even traditional Balinese dancing. Adjacent to Mal Bali Galeria is Galeria 21, the on-site movie theater. The mall welcomes visitors daily from 9 a.m. to 10 p.m., promising a vibrant shopping experience.

3. Discovery Shopping Mall

Situated conveniently along the Kuta Beach shoreline, Discovery Shopping Mall presents a haven for shoppers. This expansive establishment boasts a sprawling shopping complex and a spacious outdoor courtyard housing an array of vendors, restaurants, and al fresco dining spaces. After shopping, visitors can seamlessly transition from the mall to the beach for relaxation.

Discovery Shopping Mall offers an extensive range of department stores and boutiques, including well-known names like Billabong, Converse, and Electronic City. Dining options range from fine restaurants to quick-service outlets like Baskin Robbins and Burger King. From jewelry to electronics, this mall caters to diverse shopping interests. Be sure to check the mall's website for information on exciting cultural events happening during your visit. The mall is operational daily from 10 a.m. to 10 p.m.

4. **Padi Art Market**

An unmissable highlight on any Bali itinerary, Padi Art Market promises an enriching experience for all who step foot within. This market offers an eclectic fusion of arts, crafts, gifts, home decor, and beauty services, all embodying the tropical essence and making for perfect vacation souvenirs.

Padi Art Market showcases locally crafted items available at reasonable prices. Friendly haggling is encouraged, providing an opportunity to secure slight discounts. The market exudes a level of sophistication and refinement that sets it apart from some street markets on the island. Shoppers can discover silkscreen canvases, handcrafted pillows, and more. Additionally, the shopping center houses salons offering nail art and hair services. Padi Art Market welcomes visitors daily from 10 a.m. to 5 p.m.

5. Deus Ex Machina, which is also recognized as the "Temple of Enthusiasm,"

For enthusiasts of sports and outdoor activities, the Deus Ex Machina – Temple of Enthusiasm is a haven for procuring stylish gear. Adorned with ultra-chic street art, the store presents an array of clothing and accessories that amplify the enjoyment of outdoor pursuits. Within its walls, guests can acquire items such as surfboards, motorcycles, paddleboards, swim shorts, art, and accessories. With more than five locations in Bali and a global presence, Deus Ex Machina is a renowned chain store.

Beyond its status as a trendy gear emporium, Deus Ex Machina – Temple of Enthusiasm houses a cafe with outdoor seating and a bar serving cold beverages, including beer. The establishment's claim to fame lies in its restoration of old motorcycles, breathing new life into them. For those seeking to acquire a new or vintage motorcycle to bring back home, this destination is worth exploring. Operating daily from 7 a.m. to midnight, it caters to early risers and night owls alike.

6. Beachwalk Shopping Center

Discover the authentic essence of Bali through shopping, dining, and entertainment at the Beachwalk Shopping Center nestled within Kuta. This indoor and outdoor shopping hub complements the beach boardwalk seamlessly. With stores like Adidas, Bath & Body Works, Batik Danar Hadi, Glow Living Beauty, and Kate Spade, the mall section offers visitors a remarkable shopping experience with reasonable prices. The spacious, airy ambiance encompasses multiple floors of shopping enjoyment.

Beyond its role as a fashionable shopping spot, the Beachwalk Shopping Center boasts a wide selection of restaurants and cafes, serving everything from burgers to bubble tea. Culinary options are distributed across various buildings on the premises. After shopping, unwind in the courtyard, reclining on bean bags and lawn furniture to soak in the sun. The mall hosts a range of programs and music events throughout the month, adding to the vibrant atmosphere. Operating hours are from 10:30 am to 10:30 pm on Sunday to Thursday, and from 10 am to midnight on Friday and Saturday.

7. Love Anchor

Nestled in Canggu, Love Anchor is a beloved evening destination for those seeking the unconventional and distinctive. This charming open-air bazaar-style market is adorned with Balinese thatched huts, offering a magical ambiance as you wander through its enchanting setup. Tucked away from the beaten path, Love Anchor draws a diverse crowd, from hippies to hipsters.

Lit by whimsical colored lights, Love Anchor hosts an array of bars, restaurants, and locally-owned shops. As visitors explore the stores for unique gifts, they can later unwind in the courtyard with a beverage in hand, indulging in people-watching. Popular among tourists of various ages, Love Anchor's operating hours are from 9 a.m. to 9 p.m. daily.

8. Sukawati Art Market

A must-visit destination for avid bargain seekers, the Sukawati Art Market serves as a hub for clothing, accessories, shoes, jewelry, and a diverse array of merchandise. Renowned for offering bulk purchases at wholesale prices, the market boasts two floors of shopping delights. Situated in the Gianyar neighborhood, it attracts numerous visitors daily.

To make the most of the substantial discounts available, visitors are encouraged to consider bulk purchasing, making it a good idea to bring along friends to share in the opportunity. Alongside wholesale goods, vendors offer a range of art, wood carvings, and traditional Balinese crafts to tourists. Operating from 6 a.m. to p.m.p.m. daily, the Sukawati Art Market presents an inviting shopping experience.

9. **Krisna Bali Souvenir Shop**

Situated in Tuban, the Krisna Bali Souvenir Shop stands as a comprehensive souvenir haven for those exploring the island. This shop features a diverse array of items, perfect for commemorating a visit to Bali. With a simple ambiance, the store showcases merchandise displayed on tables and racks throughout its space.

Visitors to Krisna Bali Souvenir Shop can discover an assortment of items including beach towels, postcards, t-shirts, sandals, tote bags, keychains, and other unique finds that distinctly reflect Bali's essence. This one-stop souvenir shop offers choices for personal purchases as well as gifts for friends and family. What's notable is that Krisna Bali Souvenir Shop operates 24 hours a day, catering to shoppers at any time.

Guidelines for Shopping in Bali

Navigating shopping experiences in Bali is akin to exploring markets worldwide; your approach can significantly influence the deals you secure. Embracing the art of haggling is not just acceptable in Bali – it's an integral part of the shopping culture. Whether you're perusing local boutiques or engaging with street vendors, here's a comprehensive guide to maximize your bargaining potential:

1. Cultivate a Friendly Demeanor: Engage vendors with respect and a genuine smile. A friendly approach creates a positive atmosphere for negotiation.

2. Bundle Purchases: Consider purchasing multiple items from the same vendor. This not

only increases your chances of getting a discount but also showcases your serious intent to buy.

3. Know the Value: Before negotiations, research the approximate value of the item you're interested in. This prevents unrealistic offers that may offend the vendor.

4. Start Reasonably: Begin negotiations with a price that's lower than what you're willing to pay, but still within a reasonable range. This sets the foundation for a constructive discussion.

5. Show Interest: Express genuine interest in the item. Vendors are more likely to work out a deal if they sense your enthusiasm.

6. Patience is Key: Bargaining can be a back-and-forth process. Remain patient and open to counteroffers while maintaining a respectful demeanor.

7. Walk Away Strategically: If the vendor isn't willing to meet your desired price, consider

walking away. This can often prompt them to offer a better deal to retain your business.

8. Consider the Bigger Picture: Remember that a small amount for you could make a significant difference for the local vendor. Be fair in your negotiations.

9. Explore Local Markets: While chain stores have fixed prices, local markets, and smaller shops are where negotiation thrives. Embrace the vibrant atmosphere of traditional markets for a unique shopping experience.

10. Use Local Phrases: A few basic phrases in the local language can go a long way. It shows your respect for the culture and can create a more personal connection with the vendor.

11. Shop Early: Visit markets and shops early in the day. Vendors may be more flexible with prices to secure the first sale of the day, which is considered lucky in many cultures.

12. Don't Forget Accessories: Negotiation isn't limited to clothing or souvenirs. Taxi fares, spa treatments, and other services can often be bargained for as well.

Remember, mastering the art of bargaining not only gets you a good deal but also allows you to engage with local traditions and create memorable interactions with the people of Bali.

Chapter 9: Nightlife and Entertainment

While Bali is renowned for its temples and cultural experiences, its nightlife truly comes alive after dark. Throughout the week, both visitors and locals flock to Bali's clubs and bars, ensuring there's something for everyone to enjoy once the sun sets.

Let's explore some of the best nightlife spots across the island!

NIGHTLIFE IN SEMINYAK, BALI

Seminyak Nightclub
Seminyak, with its exquisite beaches, is a hub for Bali's nightlife. Here are some top recommendations:

1. **La Favela:** This unique indoor-outdoor bar transforms from a dining venue to a dancefloor

after 10 p.m. With international DJs and vibrant music, it's a lively spot until 3 a.m.

2. **Motel Mexicola:** Indulge in Mexican cuisine followed by a lively party and dancing. Situated in Seminyak's heart, this venue offers a Latin soundtrack and tempting tequila shots.

3. **Woo Bar:** Nestled within the elegant W Hotel, this poolside bar includes an underground counterpart called Woohouse. Groove to house and techno tunes until late into the night.

4. **Mirror Lounge and Bar**: DJs from around the globe spin tracks in this glitzy venue. With a glass roof, you can revel under the night sky while dancing away.

5. **Potato Head Beach Club**: This well-known day club has hosted renowned artists. It offers private beds and an impressive cocktail menu, complemented by captivating art installations.

While Bali offers a vibrant social scene, it's essential to be aware of the following:

- **Drug Laws**: The possession and use of drugs are illegal in Bali. It's important to avoid any involvement in such activities and distance yourself from any such behavior.

- **Personal Safety**: Solo travelers, especially women, should exercise caution and stay vigilant. Bali is a friendly place to meet new people, but it's advisable to stay cautious and be mindful of your surroundings.

- **Social Interactions**: While Bali is a wonderful place to make connections, it's worth noting that some Bali women may be involved in sex work. It's wise to be discerning about the company you keep to avoid any untoward situations.

By staying informed and prioritizing your safety, you can enjoy Bali's nightlife while making lasting memories.

NIGHTLIFE IN KUTA, BALI

Kuta Bali Bounty Nightclub

Kuta appeals to a younger crowd and boasts numerous mega-clubs that play mainstream music. It's a haven for backpackers seeking a vibrant nightlife scene. Here are some noteworthy spots in Kuta:

1. **Bounty**: Known as one of the most famous party destinations, Bounty is a dynamic nightclub in Kuta. It hosts lively wet and wild parties, drawing a youthful holidaymaker crowd. Expect unique entertainment like dancers in bird cages, drag queen shows, and exciting foam parties.

2. **Hard Rock Cafe Kuta**: Combining great food with rock and roll vibes, Hard Rock Cafe is a short stroll from Kuta Beach. Enjoy delicious meals while soaking in the energetic atmosphere.

3. **Sky Garden**: This multilevel club nestled in Kuta is one of Bali's largest nightclubs. With

distinct floors catering to diverse musical tastes, it provides an expansive space for dance enthusiasts.

4. **Boshe VVIP Club**: Situated about three kilometers from Kuta Beach, Boshe VVIP Club is an entertainment hub featuring private karaoke rooms and a spacious clubbing area. Experience pulsating strobe lights, lasers, talented DJs, and live performances.

NIGHTLIFE IN ULUWATU, BALI

1. **Single Fin:** A favorite among surfers and locals, Single Fin is renowned for its sunset views. Overlooking the sea, its expansive balcony offers delightful cocktails and wines, creating a serene atmosphere.

2. **Rock Bar:** Nestled within Ayana Resort, Rock Bar boasts breathtaking views, positioned fourteen meters above the ocean. This upscale bar provides a luxurious ambiance, along with a tempting tapas menu and live DJ performances.

3. **Karma Beach Club Bali**: Recognized as one of the world's finest beach bars, Karma Beach Club offers a stylish, beachfront setting. With beach cabanas and a restaurant, it's an ideal spot for evening drinks or dancing by the shore.

Each of these nightlife venues in Kuta and Uluwatu contributes to Bali's vibrant after-dark scene, offering a variety of experiences for all kinds of revelers.

NIGHTLIFE IN CANGGU, BALI

Amid Canggu's laid-back ambiance, nightlife options have been on the rise, echoing Kuta's famous atmosphere. Here are some of the best options for a memorable night out:

1. **Old Man's:** Situated along the beachfront, Old Man's offers international DJs and hosts the lively Dirty Ol' Wednesday parties. While it maintains a relaxed atmosphere with acoustic

sets, other nights feature energetic scratch and dance music.

2. **Sandbar**: Nestled near Old Man's, Sandbar may appear quiet during the day, but it transforms into a vibrant hotspot by night, especially on Wednesdays, Fridays, Saturdays, and Sundays. Prepare for a spirited night out!

3. **The Lawn**: Fridays at The Lawn are particularly popular, kicking off with a happy hour from 8 to 10 p.m. The night unfolds with fantastic DJs and Fridays are known for their captivating R&B music.

NIGHTLIFE IN UBUD, BALI

1. **Bar Luna:** For a sophisticated evening, Bar Luna is a top choice, hosting writers' nights and featuring live bands. Jazz enthusiasts will delight in the variety of jazz artists and guitar performances.

2. **Casa Luna**: Renowned for its Brazilian jazz night on Wednesdays at 7:30 p.m., Casa Luna offers exotic cocktails alongside Mediterranean cuisine for a refined experience.

3. **CP Lounge Ubud**: Look no further for a nightclub experience in Ubud. Serving as the city's primary late-night party venue, it boasts a live band and a bustling restaurant scene.

4. **Laughing Buddha Bar**: A must-visit for live music aficionados, Laughing Buddha Bar offers international cuisine and lively performances every night. Its roadside seating on Jalan Monkey Forest Road is perfect for people-watching.

From the vibrant energy of Canggu to the cultural heartbeat of Ubud, Bali's nightlife caters to diverse tastes. Remember to prioritize safety and avoid any involvement with drugs for a fantastic and secure night out. Embrace the captivating sunsets and unique club experiences that this stunning island has to offer! Whether you're a backpacker or a local, the nights in Bali are meant to be cherished with drinks, new friends, and dancing until dawn.

Chapter 10: Practical Tips for Travelers

1. Safe Water Consumption: As the tap water in Bali is untreated, it's advisable to avoid it to prevent stomach issues. Opt for bottled water or bring along a travel water purifier.

2. Protection from Mosquitoes: Shield yourself from mosquito-borne diseases like Dengue Fever by using strong insect repellent, especially near water bodies or during evenings.

3. Essential Vaccinations: Make sure you're up-to-date with required travel vaccines before your Bali trip, as additional immunizations might be necessary beyond your regular ones.

4. Stray Animal Caution: Steer clear of approaching stray animals to reduce the risk of exposure to rabies, which is a concern in Indonesia.

5. Dealing with Barking Dogs: Though dogs might bark, they usually won't chase you beyond their territory. Ignore them and continue walking.

6. Monkey Interaction: Exercise caution when interacting with monkeys at places like "Monkey Forests." Follow guidelines to prevent aggressive behavior and potential bites.

7. Prescription Medication: Stock up on necessary prescription medications before your trip, as sending such items by mail can be problematic.

8. Using Scooter Taxis: Instead of renting a scooter, opt for scooter taxis (like GoRide) to navigate Bali's traffic safely and efficiently.

9. Scooter Safety Measures: Always wear a helmet when riding a scooter and consider wearing protective clothing for added safety.

10. Travel Insurance: Invest in travel insurance such as SafetyWing to ensure you're covered for unexpected situations during your travels.

11. Extended Stays: If you're planning to stay in Bali for a while, consider using a travel water purifier to minimize the use of plastic bottles and reduce environmental impact.

12. Ice in Drinks Precaution: Exercise caution with ice in less frequented areas, as some places might not use filtered water for making ice. Opt for drinks without ice to avoid potential health risks.

13. Earthquake Awareness: Bali is susceptible to earthquakes. Familiarize yourself with safety procedures and stay vigilant, especially if you encounter tremors during your visit.

14. Visa Information: Non-ASEAN nationals should be aware of the need to purchase a Visa On Arrival (VOA) upon entering Indonesia. You

can extend the initial one-month VOA to two months through visa services in Bali.

15. Proof of Onward Travel: Ensure you have evidence of onward travel when entering Indonesia. Utilize services like Onward Ticket to fulfill this requirement by booking and canceling an outbound flight.

16. WhatsApp for Communication: Before arriving in Bali, download WhatsApp and link it to your phone number. This versatile app is widely used for communication and can help you stay connected throughout your trip.

17. Phone Registration: If your stay in Indonesia goes beyond three consecutive months, remember to register your phone at the airport to avoid potential taxes or SIM card deactivation.

18. Tourist SIM Card: Upon arrival, consider purchasing an Indonesian SIM card for easy communication. Opting for a "tourist SIM" will

suit your temporary usage needs during your stay.

19. Language Barrier: The widespread usage of English and the phonetic nature of Bahasa Indonesian make communication relatively straightforward in Bali.

20. Offline Google Translate: Download the Bahasa Indonesian language pack on Google Translate for offline use. This ensures effective communication even in areas with limited network service.

21. Explore Local Cuisine: Don't let the worry of "Bali Belly" prevent you from savoring Balinese food. Embrace dishes like Nasi Goreng, Mie Goreng, Nasi Campur, and Babi Guling.

22. Food Delivery Convenience: Make the most of the Gojek app's "GoFood" feature to order food delivery anytime. Alternatively, you can use the Grab app for this service.

23. Understand Local Prices: Being aware of local pricing will help you assess reasonable costs and negotiate effectively, especially with taxis and street vendors.

24. Avoid Tourist Traps: Exercise caution with Western-style or health-focused eateries, as some might be geared toward tourists. Research online reviews and explore diverse options for the best dining experiences.

25. Budget Flexibility: Be prepared for price variations in Bali, where spending can range from low to high depending on where you make purchases. Note that foreign tourists might encounter different pricing from locals.

26. Online Shopping Convenience: Although Indonesia doesn't have Amazon Prime, you can use local online platforms like Tokopedia to order various products, including supplements and prescription medications.

27. Cash Is King: As cash is the primary mode of payment in Indonesia, carry enough with you. While some places accept cards, expect cash to be the preferred method for services like tours, taxis, and meals.

28. Foreign Credit Card Challenges: Many Indonesian websites and apps may not accept foreign credit cards. To circumvent this, use non-Indonesian platforms for booking services in advance.

29. Utilize GoPay: Set up GoPay within the Gojek app to conveniently pay for rides, services, and online purchases. It's an efficient option for transactions and works with an Indonesian SIM card.

30. Small Bills Count: Hang on to smaller bills, as obtaining change might be challenging in certain situations. Carrying smaller denominations will prove useful when change is needed.

31. Service and Tax Charges: It's important to be mindful of mandatory service and tax charges at many tourist-oriented restaurants. Typically ranging around 10% for tax and 5-10% for service, these charges negate the need for additional tipping.

32. Ride-Hailing Apps Convenience: Download apps like GoJek or Grab to simplify your transportation needs in Bali. These apps encompass ride-hailing, food delivery, and payment services.

33. Beyond Urban Centers: While ride-sharing apps work well within city limits, securing a ride back from more remote areas can pose challenges. For journeys outside city boundaries, hiring a private driver for day trips is a viable option.

34. Beware of Taxi Mafia: Exercise caution around the Taxi Mafia, a group of taxi drivers aiming to oust ride-sharing apps in tourist hubs.

To steer clear of potential issues, opt for private drivers or alternative transportation methods.

35. Handling Street Approaches: Street vendors might approach you frequently, but a simple "no thank you" is usually sufficient. Wearing headphones and minimizing eye contact can help deter unwelcome interactions.

36. Interpreting Honking: Honking in Bali conveys a cautionary message rather than aggression. It's a means for drivers to alert others to their presence, especially in narrow pathways.

37. Embrace Traditional Guesthouses: Opting for family-run traditional guesthouses brings benefits like cost-effectiveness, personalized attention, and a chance to immerse in Balinese culture.

38. Explore Diverse Areas: Bali's various regions offer unique atmospheres. Don't confine yourself to one locale—venture to Canggu for a

digital nomad scene, Kuta for surfing and nightlife, and Ubud for its spiritual ambiance.

39. Consider Hostels: Hostels are ideal for solo travelers to connect with like-minded individuals. Bali's hostels maintain high standards, providing social opportunities and economical accommodations.

40. Luxury Delights: Enhance your experience with a touch of luxury by treating yourself to an upscale encounter in Bali. From infinity pools to Balinese spas, esteemed hotels like Amandari in Ubud and Bulgari Resort in Uluwatu offer unforgettable stays.

Elevate your Bali sojourn by selecting fitting accommodations, and transportation options, and immersing yourself in the diverse range of experiences this captivating island has to offer.

41. Luxurious Treat on a Budget: Pamper yourself with Bali's renowned spas and luxury offerings, even if you're watching your expenses.

Choose services with positive online reviews to ensure a satisfying indulgence.

42. Embrace Your Tourist Role: Don't hesitate to embrace your tourist identity in Bali. The destination's popularity as a top tourist hub is well-deserved.

43. Respectful Visitor Etiquette: While being a tourist is acceptable, respecting the local culture is crucial. Refrain from disrespecting sacred ceremonies and offerings.

44. Consider Organized Excursions: Opt for organized tours to make the most of your Bali vacation, especially if time is limited. This approach minimizes stress and maximizes your experience.

45. Realistic Expectations: While Bali is incredible, don't be disheartened if famed spots don't live up to their online hype. Often, hidden gems surpass overhyped locations.

46. Early Arrival for Serenity: To avoid crowds at popular sites like Bali's Sunrise Gate of Heaven, arrive early. Alternatively, hire a private driver for a more personalized exploration.

47. Uncover Hidden Gems: Google Maps can lead you to Bali's lesser-known treasures that aren't plastered all over Instagram.

48. Private Driver or Self-Drive: Consider hiring a private driver or driving yourself to tourist attractions for a flexible and crowd-free adventure.

49. Venture Beyond Bali: Extend your exploration to neighboring islands like Java or the serene beaches of the Gili Islands. Don't restrict your adventures to Bali alone.

50. Remember "Bagus": Familiarize yourself with the Indonesian term "Bagus," which signifies "good." Beyond its literal meaning, it encompasses a broader sense of positivity and enjoyment.

Chapter 11: Guide To Lombok

Lombok often remains overlooked and bypassed in many travelers' Indonesian itineraries. Positioned as Bali's larger neighbor, Lombok offers a more mountainous and less crowded environment, still retaining its allure as a surfer's haven. Picture dense green jungles, towering waterfalls, breathtaking vistas overlooking rice fields, and nearly untouched beaches – that's Lombok in a nutshell.

Sounds like a dream, doesn't it? If you're someone who seeks to stray from the well-trodden path, consider skipping a few Bali attractions and setting your sights on Lombok or perhaps even venturing further to Flores. While Lombok isn't entirely off the radar, it draws significantly fewer visitors compared to Bali, and it's home to the renowned Gili Islands.

To be honest, Lombok wasn't my personal favorite among Indonesia's islands, primarily due to higher transportation costs and the experience of locals not being as friendly as on other Indonesian islands. However, please note that this was my perspective, and I've provided more details below to ensure you're well-prepared cost-wise. Many people adore Lombok, especially if they're avid surfers.

Trust me, Lombok is worth exploring if you have a penchant for natural landscapes, trekking, waterfalls, and beaches! However, the true essence of the island can only be experienced through your journey to Lombok.

Keep in mind that all prices mentioned are in Indonesian rupiah.

Navigating Your Way To Lombok

Getting to Lombok presents several options to choose from:

Traveling from Bali to Lombok:

1. Flight: Opt for a quick 30-minute flight from Bali to Lombok's only airport, situated in the southern region of Kuta.

2. Boat: Alternatively, consider a boat journey. Public ferries operate from Bali's Padang Bai Harbour and arrive at Lembar Harbour in Lombok (near Senggigi). The ferry ride typically takes around 4-5 hours, departing every hour. Tickets, priced at 46,000 Indonesian rupiah per person, are available for purchase at the harbor. Note that prices may vary.

3. Fast Boat: Another option is the fast boat, which takes approximately 2 hours. Be sure to research thoroughly before booking, as the reputation of fast boats in Bali can be inconsistent. Prices range from USD 35+.

Traveling from Gili Islands to Lombok:

1. Public Boats: To reach Lombok's Bangsal Harbour from any of the Gili Islands, you can utilize public boats. These boats are relatively affordable, costing less than 20,000 Indonesian rupiah. Travel times vary based on your departure island, with Gili T being the farthest away at approximately 40 minutes. Keep in mind that these boats usually wait until they're full before departing.

2. Fast Boat: The second option is to take a fast boat, which tends to be pricier (around 80,000 Indonesian rupiah). Tickets can be acquired from numerous tourist shops on any of the islands.

Transportation Options In Lombok

Getting around Lombok is reminiscent of Bali's transportation landscape. Just like in Bali, public transport is not widely available in Lombok. While Bali has GoJek for affordable rides, Lombok doesn't offer this service. Instead, traveling between destinations in Lombok necessitates hiring private drivers, which can be quite expensive. For instance, I paid 500,000 Indonesian rupiah for a 2.5-hour drive from Sembalun in the north to Kuta in the south.

From places like Kuta and Senggigi, shared buses are accessible at stalls along the main streets. Additionally, transfers are often included in Rinjani tour packages originating from Kuta or the harbor.

To reach waterfalls and beaches, arranging private cars or embarking on self-driven day trips becomes essential. Sharing the cost of a car with friends can be a cost-effective solution for these excursions.

Renting a bike is an option for Lombok exploration, but it's important to be prepared for lengthy rides or rental restrictions for extended journeys. An alternative approach is to rent a bike in Bali and then transport it to Lombok via the public ferry (the only means to bring a bike).

This way, you can enjoy cruising around Lombok's picturesque landscapes.

Lombok Itinerary

Customizing your ideal Lombok itinerary depends on your preferences, but I recommend setting aside a minimum of one week to fully immerse yourself in Lombok and its captivating Gili Islands. If you're aiming for a more comprehensive experience, extending your stay to 10 days would offer an enriching exploration. The following itineraries outline the destinations to visit in Lombok and suggest an optimal timeframe for each. Feel free to adjust the pace to match your desired level of relaxation.

Lombok 7-Day Itinerary

Senggigi: Days 1-2
Kick off your journey in the charming coastal town of Senggigi. Explore its scenic beaches, and vibrant markets, and indulge in fresh

seafood. Enjoy strolls along the coastline, witnessing stunning sunsets that paint the sky with captivating hues.

Senaru - Waterfalls & Villages: Days 3-4
Venture inland to Senaru, where you'll be greeted by picturesque waterfalls and traditional villages. Immerse yourself in the beauty of Tiu Kelep and Sendang Gile waterfalls, followed by cultural experiences in local villages.

Kuta: Days 5-7

Conclude your week in Kuta, a lively hub known for its stunning beaches and vibrant surf culture. Spend your days catching waves, exploring nearby beaches like Tanjung Aan, and savoring local cuisine. Kuta offers a mix of relaxation and excitement, making it a perfect ending to your Lombok experience.

Lombok 10-Day Itinerary
Senggigi: Days 1-2

Extend your stay in Senggigi to fully embrace its relaxed coastal vibe. Take time to explore hidden gems, engage with locals, and enjoy the serene ambiance.

Senaru - Waterfalls & Villages: Days 3-4

Delve deeper into Senaru, discovering more waterfalls and engaging with the culture and traditions of the Sasak people. Explore the vibrant local life and partake in activities like rice farming.

Kuta: Days 5-7

Return to Kuta for more beach adventures, surf sessions, and opportunities to explore nearby beaches. Delight in the nightlife scene, sampling local dishes and experiencing the energetic atmosphere.

Gili Islands: Days 8-10

Embark on a short boat ride to the captivating Gili Islands. Spend your days island-hopping, snorkeling, and reveling in the serene beauty of Gili Trawangan, Gili Air, and Gili Meno.

Activities in Lombok by Region

Senggigi: Relax on idyllic beaches, shop at vibrant markets, and unwind with sunset views. Engage in water sports, and hiking, and immerse yourself in the local culture.

Senaru - Waterfalls & Villages: Discover stunning waterfalls like Tiu Kelep and Sendang Gile. Engage with the Sasak community, learn about traditional weaving, and experience the daily life of villagers.

Kuta: Enjoy the surf culture, and pristine beaches, and indulge in mouthwatering seafood. Explore the nearby Tanjung Aan Beach, visit local markets, and embrace the lively nightlife.

Gili Islands: Snorkel in crystal-clear waters, go diving and experience the unique charm of each Gili Island. Relax on the white sandy beaches, dine at beachfront restaurants, and enjoy vibrant night scenes.

Crafting your Lombok itinerary provides the chance to immerse yourself in diverse experiences and create lasting memories in this Indonesian paradise.

Exploring Northern Lombok

Senaru and Sembulan

Discover the mountain towns of Senaru and Sembulan, nestled at the base of the majestic Rinjani volcano. While Senaru is the more popular of the two, serving as a common starting point for Rinjani treks, Sembulan also offers access to this stunning natural wonder, making it a convenient alternative for trekkers. Here are some remarkable activities to engage in while in these regions:

Trekking Rinjani

Embark on a thrilling adventure by trekking the iconic Rinjani volcano. Note that this is no ordinary trek; it's a challenging endeavor best suited for experienced hikers. Two- to three-day treks involve intense 7-8-hour daily treks across uneven terrain. You'll start with a demanding 1500m ascent over 8km. While it's an arduous journey, it rewards trekkers with breathtaking views. Opt for two-day treks leading to the summit or crater rim, or extend to three days to include a lake visit and relaxation in the natural hot springs of Rinjani.

Sendang Gile Waterfall

Delight in the beauty of Sendang Gile Waterfall, a magnificent sight that promises fantastic Instagram-worthy moments. Easily accessible from Senaru, this towering waterfall graces the main town. While locals may offer guide services for a fee, you can navigate the obvious path to Sendang Gile independently. A small entrance fee of 10,000 IDR covers access to both Sendang Gile and Tiu Kelep waterfalls.

Tiu Kelep Waterfall

A visit to Lombok isn't complete without witnessing the breathtaking Tiu Kelep Waterfall. The moderately easy trail leads to this stunning cascade, making it accessible to most visitors. Tiu Kelep surpasses even Sendang Gile in grandeur. After descending the stairs, you'll encounter a second path to the left that leads to Tiu Kelep. Local children may offer to guide you for a small fee of around 20,000 IDR. Their assistance is valuable for capturing photos and navigating water crossings, which are shallow and pose no challenge.

Travel Tips for Waterfall Visits

For a more serene experience, plan your waterfall visits on weekdays, avoiding the weekend crowds, especially on Sundays. This way, you'll have the opportunity to appreciate the beauty of these natural wonders without the hustle and bustle.

Unveil the beauty of North Lombok as you engage in captivating adventures, from conquering Rinjani's trails to marveling at the awe-inspiring Sendang Gile and Tiu Kelep waterfalls.

In addition to the well-known attractions, North Lombok offers a treasure trove of hidden gems that promise unique and fulfilling experiences. Venture beyond the beaten path to uncover these remarkable spots:

Tiu Teja Waterfall

While I did not have the chance to explore Tiu Teja Waterfall, it stands as another captivating destination in the northern part of Lombok. Conveniently situated near Santong village, this jungle oasis can be visited en route to or from Senaru or Senggigi, which is approximately an hour away. Its remote location adds to the allure of this natural wonder, nestled amidst lush surroundings.

Trek Perigasingan Hill

For those seeking an active adventure without the rigor of the Rinjani trek, consider ascending Perigasingan Hill in Sembalun. This soft trek offers a 2-3 hour round trip and is ideal for sunrise viewing, providing stunning vistas of Rinjani as the sun graces the horizon. Although not categorized as an easy trek due to segments with a 70° incline and loose rocks, it's certainly manageable for most. This is where Rinjani porters train, further adding to its allure. The trek can also be undertaken as an overnight journey, allowing you to avoid the dark ascent.

Embark on this journey with appropriate preparation, as even though it's relatively short, the cost can be substantial. I secured a private tour through my Senaru accommodation for 800,000 IDR, inclusive of lunch and transfers, which was the most budget-friendly option I found.

Bukit Selong Rice Field Viewpoint

Discover the breathtaking beauty of Bukit Selong Rice Field Viewpoint, a place that will undoubtedly captivate your senses. This viewpoint, located in Sembalun, offers one of the most stunning perspectives of rice fields I've ever encountered. As you gaze into the distance, the enchanting Perigasingan Hill beckons. Although the Perigasingan trek also offers views of these rice fields, this viewpoint grants a unique angle.

With a modest entrance fee of 10,000 IDR, you'll embark on a short 10-minute hike to reach the viewpoint. Upon arrival, veer to the right at the top of the stairs to discover a star-adorned area. Just beyond this point lies a weathered yet charming bridge that affords panoramic views of Sembalun's scenic landscapes.

Incorporate these lesser-known destinations into your North Lombok itinerary to uncover the hidden treasures that this region has to offer.

Things To Do In Central Lombok

Waterfall Haven

While central Lombok may not offer a wide array of attractions, it boasts some captivating waterfalls that are well worth a visit. Instead of considering it as a place to stay, I recommend incorporating these waterfalls into your itinerary as part of your journey from Senaru, Sembulan, or even as a day trip from Kuta.

Benang Stokel and Benang Kelambu Waterfalls

Nestled in the heart of central Lombok, Air Berik is home to the enchanting Benang Stokel and Benang Kelambu Waterfalls. Although there are a total of 5 waterfalls in the area, these two are deemed the most remarkable. (Unfortunately, I didn't have the chance to explore the other three, but let's focus on these two gems!)

Begin your journey with Bengang Stokel, a mere 5-minute walk from the entrance. As you follow the left path, you'll be greeted by a captivating double waterfall. The picturesque setting offers an ideal backdrop for photographs without even needing to step into the water.

For an even more enchanting experience, proceed to my personal favorite, Benang Kelambu waterfall. A 15-20 minute walk from Benang Stokel, this waterfall transports you to a fairytale realm, where water gently cascades from lush greenery. As you journey back towards the entrance, a path with stairs on the right leads you to this magical spot.

Upon arrival, local guides may direct you to an office, where they might propose a guide fee of 150,000 IDR or 60,000 IDR to access each waterfall. Haggling is not uncommon, and my friend and I secured entry without a guide for 50,000 IDR each. While you may want a guide for the less prominent waterfalls, I chose to explore them independently.

Easily accessible on a day trip from Kuta, these waterfalls are approximately a 2-hour drive away. However, I strongly advise against relying solely on Google Maps for navigation, unless you're fond of traversing rocky farmers' paths. Instead, opt for Maps. me, an app offering offline maps that can guide you to the correct location.

Kuta Lombok: Surfers' Haven and Beyond

Kuta Lombok beckons surf enthusiasts with its pristine waves and serene shores, making it an idyllic paradise for beach lovers. Serving as the gateway with its airport, Kuta can be an excellent starting or concluding point for your Lombok escapade.

Merges Hill (Sunset Point)

Captivating both locals and tourists, Merges Hill offers an unparalleled vantage point to witness the sun gracefully dip behind the hills. Within a quick 10-minute hike, you'll reach the pinnacle, where the captivating sunset views unfold. Conveniently situated near Tanjung Aan beach, you can seamlessly combine a visit to both attractions in a single day, as they are merely a 20-minute drive outside the main town.

Embrace the allure of central Lombok's waterfalls and immerse yourself in the surfers' haven of Kuta to craft a captivating and diverse Lombok experience.

Explore the Coastal Beauty of Kuta Lombok

Tanjung Aan Beach: A Serene Oasis
Among the collection of picturesque beaches in Kuta, Tanjung Aan stands out as my personal favorite. What truly captivated me were its tranquil cerulean waters and the well-developed ambiance it offers. Along the shore, bamboo lounge chairs provide comfortable seating, while unassuming restaurants beckon you to savor a

refreshing coconut or a delectable lunch without ever leaving the beach.

The more developed nature of Tanjung Aan also means that local vendors, including children, may approach you to sell their wares, such as sarongs, pineapples, and bracelets. While their persistence might be more than necessary, being prepared for such interactions will enhance your experience.

A roughly 20-minute drive from the main town, the journey to Tanjung Aan is mostly smooth, with the last stretch featuring some potholes. These minor road inconveniences are far outweighed by the beauty that awaits you.

Batu Puyung Rock Formation: A Natural Marvel

Close to Tanjung Aan beach lies the intriguing Batu Puyung Rock Formation, resembling an umbrella. This unique rock formation can be accessed for a memorable photo opportunity by either boat from the beach or on foot. Opting for the walk takes approximately an hour, leading you across rocky terrain and enchanting rock pools. The solitude of this experience, with the possibility of being the only one traversing this route, adds to its allure.

Kuta Beach: Lombok's Bustling Hub

Serving as the primary beach near Kuta, Lombok, Kuta Beach boasts a stretch of inviting sand and gentle waves, ideal for swimming. The local flavor is palpable, as food stalls offer refreshing drinks and light snacks. While Kuta Beach is popular among locals, it maintains a refreshing sense of space compared to Bali's crowded beaches. A nominal parking fee of 10,000 IDR is charged.

Mawun Beach: Secluded Serenity

A 20-minute drive from the main town, Mawun Beach enchants with its tranquility. The journey leads you over rolling hills and through breathtaking viewpoints perfect for scenic snapshots. While waves here are larger, creating a more dynamic environment, bamboo lounge chairs and beachside eateries provide a cozy setting for relaxation. The ongoing construction along the route might pose some inconvenience, but rapid improvements are transforming the roads.

Pink Beach: A Hidden Gem

Located about an hour's drive from Kuta, Pink Beach exudes a unique charm. While the sand itself may not be vividly pink, a subtle pink hue graces the beach. Engaging in water activities like snorkeling, diving, or island hopping adds to the allure of this quiet haven. The crystalline waters beckon you for a refreshing swim, while a hillside vantage point offers sweeping views of the shoreline.

Embark on a coastal adventure in Kuta Lombok, where each beach offers a distinctive charm, from tranquil shores to captivating rock formations, ensuring your exploration is as diverse as it is enchanting.

Ride the Waves and Find Inner Peace

Surfing Adventures in Kuta, Lombok

Kuta, Lombok is renowned as a surfing haven in Indonesia. Unlike Bali, it remains untouched by excessive tourism, presenting surf enthusiasts with an idyllic setting to ride the waves without overwhelming crowds. While I might not be an expert on the best spots or surfing techniques, I can certainly encourage you to explore this captivating realm further through dedicated research.

Yoga Oasis in Kuta

Kuta is transforming into a yoga haven, akin to the famed Canggu. Amidst your beach explorations or exhilarating surf sessions, indulge in a zen experience at one of the two existing yoga studios in Kuta. Both Mana Retreat & Yoga and Ashtari Lombok offer walk-in yoga classes along with package deals for those looking for a more immersive practice.

The beauty of the surroundings and the quality of instruction were truly exceptional. Ashtari Lombok, with its multiple class locations, including a hilltop setting, presents a breathtaking backdrop for your yoga journey.

Sunset Delights at Ashtari

Ashtari, a stunning hilltop establishment, not only offers yoga classes but also boasts a restaurant. Whether you partake in a yoga session or not, visiting Ashtari rewards you with panoramic views from its elevated vantage point. A sunset experience here is a must, even though it might not rival the grandeur of Merek Hill. While the prices align with typical Western-style restaurants in Indonesia, the delectable food and picturesque surroundings make it a cherished spot.

Culinary Delights at El Bazar

Incorporating culinary experiences into travel guides isn't my norm, but the charm of El Bazar compelled me to make an exception. Its Instagram-worthy ambiance is captivating, particularly the back terrace, which sadly closes for dinner. To bask in its delightful aura, visit during the day. Take a glimpse at the adorable picture above! While it's relatively higher priced, it's not exorbitant, and the taste of the food makes every bite worth it.

Embrace the Essence of Kuta

From conquering the waves to finding solace in yoga, Kuta, Lombok offers an array of experiences that encapsulate the spirit of the island. Whether you're drawn to the allure of surfing or the serenity of yoga, the beauty of Kuta welcomes you to explore and discover your version of paradise.

Accommodation Options In Lombok

Embarking on your Lombok adventure requires the perfect place to rest your head. Whether you're seeking budget-friendly options, mid-range comfort, or the lap of luxury, Lombok offers a range of accommodations to suit your preferences.

Senaru:

As the starting point for those conquering Mount Rinjani, Senaru provides a variety of lodging options to suit different budgets.

Budget: Rinjani Trails Hotel
Ideal for trekkers and budget-conscious travelers, the Rinjani Trails Hotel offers a comfortable stay without breaking the bank. It's a great place to rest before or after your Rinjani adventure.

Mid-Range: Dragonfly Senaru Lodge
For a more comfortable stay with a touch of local charm, the Dragonfly Senaru Lodge provides a mid-range option that balances affordability with quality service.

Luxury: Rinjani Lodge
Elevate your Senaru experience with a stay at the luxurious Rinjani Lodge. This indulgent accommodation option adds a touch of sophistication to your mountainous retreat.

Kuta:

Kuta serves as both the entry and exit point of your Lombok journey, making your choice of lodging here crucial to your overall experience.

Budget: Bamba Capsule Hostel
Experience Kuta's vibrant atmosphere with the affordability and camaraderie offered by Bamba Capsule Hostel. A great choice for budget travelers seeking a sociable environment.

Mid-Range: Aldi's Bungalow and Homestay
Nestled in the heart of Kuta, Aldi's Bungalow and Homestay provides comfortable mid-range accommodations, allowing you to immerse yourself in the local culture.

Luxury: Kies Villas Lombok
For those seeking opulence, Kies Villas Lombok offers a luxurious haven complete with modern amenities, ensuring a lavish stay amidst the island's beauty.

Senggigi:

If you find yourself transitioning through Senggigi, consider staying for a night to explore this coastal town.

Budget: Selasar Hostel
Enjoy Senggigi's serene ambiance without breaking the bank at Selasar Hostel. It offers budget-friendly lodgings, perfect for a peaceful night's rest.

Mid-Range: Kebun Villas & Resort
Indulge in the lush surroundings of Senggigi with a mid-range stay at Kebun Villas & Resort. Unwind amidst nature while relishing in modern comforts.

Luxury: Katamaran Hotel & Resort
For a touch of luxury, the Katamaran Hotel & Resort provides a refined escape by the sea. Pamper yourself with impeccable service and upscale facilities.

Gili Islands: Tropical Paradise

Extend your Lombok adventure by visiting the renowned Gili Islands, offering idyllic beaches and crystal-clear waters.

Budget: Gili La Boheme
In Gili Trawangan, Gili La Boheme presents cozy accommodations with a budget-friendly price tag, allowing you to experience the island's vibrant atmosphere.

Mid-Range: Pearl of Trawangan
For a comfortable stay in proximity to Gili Trawangan's attractions, Pearl of Trawangan offers a blend of relaxation and adventure.

Luxury: Vila Ombak

Indulge in the epitome of luxury at Vila Ombak, Gili Trawangan's prominent resort. Experience exquisite accommodations, stunning pools, and direct access to the beach.

Whichever accommodation you choose, your Lombok trip promises unforgettable moments. Explore the island's stunning landscapes, immerse yourself in local culture, and find solace in your chosen home away from home. From serene coastal towns to vibrant beaches, Lombok invites you to experience its diverse beauty and embrace the tranquility of its surroundings.

Printed in Great Britain
by Amazon

30769589R00123